TEACHER'S GUIDE

DAYBOOK

. . . .

of Critical Reading and Writing

daybook, *n.* a book in which the events of the day are recorded; *specif.* a journal or diary

GRADE 8

CONSULTING AUTHORS

FRAN CLAGGETT

LOUANN REID

RUTH VINZ

Great Source Education Group
a Houghton Mifflin Company
Wilmington, Massachusetts

www.greatsource.com

Consulting Authors

Fran Claggett, currently an educational consultant for schools throughout the country and teacher at Sonoma State University, taught high school English for more than thirty years. She is author of several books, including *Drawing Your Own Conclusions: Graphic Strategies for Reading, Writing, and Thinking* (1992) and *A Measure of Success* (1996).

Louann Reid taught junior and senior high school English, speech, and drama for nineteen years and currently teaches courses for future English teachers at Colorado State University. Author of numerous articles and chapters, her first books were *Learning the Landscape* and *Recasting the Text* with Fran Claggett and Ruth Vinz (1996).

Ruth Vinz, currently a professor and director of English education at Teachers College, Columbia University, taught in secondary schools for twenty-three years. She is author of several books and numerous articles that discuss teaching and learning in the English classroom as well as a frequent presenter, consultant, and co-teacher in schools throughout the country.

Printed in the United States of America

International Standard Book Number: 0-669-46790-1

5 6 7 8 9 10 -POO- 04 03 02 01

Great Source wishes to acknowledge the many insights and improvements made to the *Daybooks* thanks to the work of the following teachers and educators.

R e a d e r s

Jay Amberg
Glenbrook South High School
Glenview, Illinois

Joanne Arellanes
Rancho Cordova, California

Nancy Bass
Moore Middle School
Arvada, Colorado

Jim Benny
Sierra Mountain Middle School
Truckee, California

Noreen Benton
Guilderland High School
Altamont, New York

Janet Bertucci
Hawthorne Junior High School
Vernon Hills, Illinois

Jim Burke
Burlingame High School
Burlingame, California

Mary Castellano
Hawthorne Junior High School
Vernon Hills, Illinois

Diego Davalos
Chula Vista High School
Chula Vista, California

Jane Detgen
Daniel Wright Middle School
Lake Forest, Illinois

Michelle Ditzian
Shepard Junior High School
Deerfield, Illinois

Jenni Dunlap
Highland Middle School
Libertyville, Illinois

Judy Elman
Highland Park High School
Highland Park, Illinois

Mary Ann Evans-Patrick
Fox Valley Writing Project
Oshkosh, Wisconsin

Howard Frishman
Twin Grove Junior High School
Buffalo Grove, Illinois

Kathleen Gaynor
Wheaton, Illinois

Beatrice Gerrish
Bell Middle School
Golden, Colorado

Kathy Glass
San Carlos, California

Alton Greenfield
Minnesota Dept. of Child,
Family & Learning
St. Paul, Minnesota

Sue Hebson
Deerfield High School
Deerfield, Illinois

Carol Jago
Santa Monica High School
Santa Monica, California

Diane Kepner
Oakland, California

Lynne Ludwig
Gregory Middle School
Naperville, Illinois

Joan Markos-Horejs
Fox Valley Writing Project
Oshkosh, Wisconsin

James McDermott
South High Community School
Worcester, Massachusetts

Tim McGee
Worland High School
Worland, Wyoming

Mary Jane Mulholland
Lynn Classical High School
Lynn, Massachusetts

Lisa Myers
Englewood, Colorado

Karen Neilsen
Desert Foothills Middle School
Phoenix, Arizona

Jayne Allen Nichols
El Camino High School
Sacramento, California

Mary Nicolini
Penn Harris High School
Mishawaka, Indiana

Lucretia Pannozzo
John Jay Middle School
Katonah, New York

Robert Pavlick
Marquette University
Milwaukee, Wisconsin

Linda Popp
Gregory Middle School
Naperville, Illinois

Caroline Ratliffe
Fort Bend Instructional School District
Sugar Land, Texas

Guerrino Rich
Akron North High School
Akron, Ohio

Shirley Rosson
Alief Instructional School District
Houston, Texas

Alan Ruter
Glenbrook South High School
Glenview, Illinois

Rene Schillenger
Washington, D.C.

Georgianne Schulte
Oak Park Middle School
Oak Park, Illinois

Carol Schultz
Tinley Park, Illinois

Wendell Schwartz
Adlai E. Stevenson High School
Lincolnshire, Illinois

Lynn Snell
Oak Grove School
Green Oaks, Illinois

Hildi Spritzer
Oakland, California

Bill Stone
Plano Senior High School
Plano, Texas

Barbara Thompson
Hazelwood School
Florissant, Missouri

Elma Torres
Orange Grove Instructional
School District
Orange Grove, Texas

Bill Weber
Libertyville High School
Libertyville, Illinois

Darby Williams
Sacramento, California

Hillary Zunin
Napa High School
Napa, California

Table of Contents

O v e r v i e w

What is a daybook and what is it good for? These are the first questions asked about this series, *Daybooks of Critical Reading and Writing.*

The answer is that a daybook is a keepable, journal-like book that helps improve students' reading and writing. *Daybooks* are a tool to promote daily reading and writing in classrooms. By immersing students in good literature and by asking them to respond creatively to it, the *Daybooks* combine critical reading and creative, personal response to literature.

The literature in each *Daybook* has been chosen to complement the selections commonly found in anthologies and the most commonly taught novels. Most of the literature selections are brief and designed to draw students into them by their brevity and high-interest appeal. In addition, each passage has a literary quality that will be probed in the lesson.

Each lesson focuses on a specific aspect of critical reading—that is, the reading skills used by good readers. These aspects of critical reading are summarized in closing statements positioned at the end of each lesson. To organize this wide-ranging analysis into critical reading, the consulting authors have constructed a framework called the "Angles of Literacy."

This framework organizes the lessons and units in the *Daybook.* The five Angles of Literacy described here are:

- marking or annotating the text
- examining the story connections
- looking at authors' perspectives
- studying the language and craft of a text
- focusing on individual authors

The Angles of Literacy are introduced in the first cluster of the *Daybook* and then explored in greater depth in subsequent clusters.

The *Daybook* concept was developed to help teachers with a number of practical concerns:

1. To introduce daily (or at least weekly) critical reading and writing into classrooms

2. To fit into the new configurations offered by block scheduling

3. To create a literature book students can own, allowing them to mark up the literature and write as they read

4. To make an affordable literature book that students can carry home

How to Use the Daybook

As the *Daybooks* were being developed, more than fifty teachers commented on and reviewed the lesson concept and individual lessons and units. Middle school teachers helped shape the choice of literature and the skills to be taught. From their efforts and our discussions, several main uses for the *Daybooks* emerged.

1. Supplementing an Anthology

For literature teachers stuck with dated anthologies, the *Daybooks* appeared to offer an easy, economical means of updating their literature curriculums. The multitude of contemporary authors and wide range of multicultural authors fit nicely with older and soon-to-become out-of-date anthology series.

2. Supplementing a List of Core Novels

For middle schools guided by a list of core readings, the *Daybooks* offered a convenient way to add some daily writing and critical reading instruction to classes. Plus, the emphasis on newer, young adult writers seemed to these teachers just right for their courses laden with "classics."

3. Adding a New Element

Some middle school teachers use the *Daybooks* to add literature to their curriculum; some use them to add an element of critical reading to what is already a literature-based approach; other teachers rely on the *Daybooks* to add the element of daily reading and writing to their curriculum. Teachers have found a number of different ways to slot the *Daybooks* into their curriculums, mostly because of their three-way combination of literature, critical reading, and daily creative writing.

4. Block Scheduling

Daybook activities were also designed to accommodate new block-scheduled class periods. With longer periods, teachers commented on the need to introduce 2–4 parts to each "block," one of which would be a *Daybook* lesson. The brief, self-contained lessons fit perfectly at the beginning or end of a block and could be used to complement or build upon another segment of the day.

The reviewers of the *Daybooks* proved that no two classrooms are alike. While each was unique in its own way, every teacher found use for the *Daybook* lessons in the classroom. In the end, the usefulness of the *Daybooks* derived from the blend of elements they alone offer:

- direct instruction of how to read critically
- regular and explicit practice in marking up and annotating texts
- "writing to learn" activities for each day or week
- great selections from contemporary (and often multicultural) literature
- in-depth instruction in how to read literature and write effectively about it

Organization of the Daybooks

Each *Daybook* has 14 units, or clusters, of five lessons. A lesson is designed to last approximately 30 minutes, although some lessons will surely extend longer depending on how energetically students attack the writing activities. But the intent throughout was to create brief, potent lessons that integrate quality literature, critical reading instruction, and writing.

The unifying concept behind these lessons is the Angles of Literacy—the idea that a selection can be approached from at least five directions:

- by annotating and marking up the text
- by analyzing the story connections in the literature
- by examining authors' perspectives
- by studying the language and craft of the writer
- by focusing closely on all of the aspects of a single writer's work

A lesson typically begins with an introduction and leads quickly into a literary selection. By looking closely at the selection, students are able to discover what can be learned through careful reading. Students are led to look again at the selection and to respond analytically, reflectively, and creatively to what they have read. An Answer Key at the back of this book provides selected sample responses.

focus on critical reading

lesson title

boldface terms in glossary

... the central point ... a piece of nonfiction.

metaphor, comparison of two unlike things without using a word of comparison such as *like* or *as*. Example: "The stars were diamonds."

... poem's rhythm

unit title

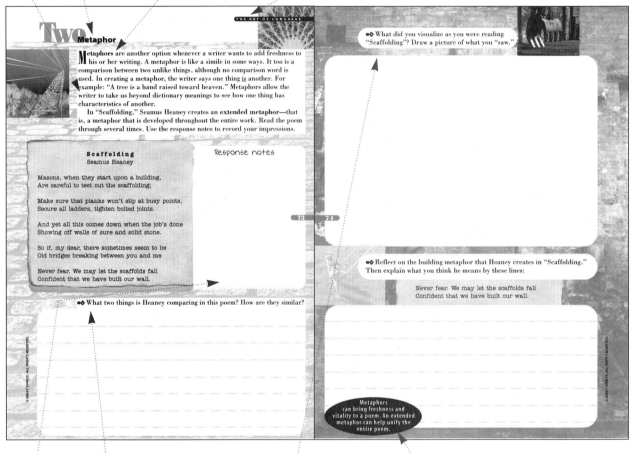

THE ART OF LANGUAGE

Two
Metaphor

Metaphors are another option whenever a writer wants to add freshness to his or her writing. A metaphor is like a simile in some ways. It too is a comparison between two unlike things, although no comparison word is used. In creating a metaphor, the writer says one thing *is* another. For example: "A tree is a hand raised toward heaven." Metaphors allow the writer to take us beyond dictionary meanings to see how one thing has characteristics of another.

In "Scaffolding," Seamus Heaney creates an extended **metaphor**—that is, a metaphor that is developed throughout the entire work. Read the poem through several times. Use the response notes to record your impressions.

Scaffolding
Seamus Heaney

Masons, when they start upon a building,
Are careful to test out the scaffolding;

Make sure that planks won't slip at busy points,
Secure all ladders, tighten bolted joints.

And yet all this comes down when the job's done
Showing off walls of sure and solid stone.

So if, my dear, there sometimes seem to be
Old bridges breaking between you and me

Never fear. We may let the scaffolds fall
Confident that we have built our wall.

Response notes

What two things is Heaney comparing in this poem? How are they similar?

What did you visualize as you were reading "Scaffolding"? Draw a picture of what you "saw."

Reflect on the building metaphor that Heaney creates in "Scaffolding." Then explain what you think he means by these lines:

Never fear. We may let the scaffolds fall
Confident that we have built our wall.

Metaphors can bring freshness and vitality to a poem. An extended metaphor can help unify the entire poem.

space for annotations

summary statement

longer, interpretive response to literature

initial response activity

F r e q u e n t l y   A s k e d   Q u e s t i o n s

One benefit of the extensive field-testing of the *Daybooks* was to highlight right at the beginning several questions about the *Daybooks*.

1. What is a daybook anyway?

A daybook used to be "a book in which daily transactions are recorded" or "a diary." Most recently, the word has been used to mean "journal." To emphasize the daily reading and writing, the authors chose the word *daybook* rather than *journal*. And, indeed, the *Daybooks* are much more than journals, in that they include literature selections and instruction in critical reading.

2. Are students supposed to write in the *Daybook*?

Yes, definitely. Only by physically marking the text will students become active readers. To interact with a text and take notes as an active reader, students must write in their *Daybooks*. Students will have a written record of their thoughts, questions, brainstorms, annotations, and creative responses. The immediacy of reading and responding on the page is an integral feature of the *Daybooks*. Students will also benefit from the notebook-like aspect, allowing them to double back to earlier work, see progress, store ideas, and record responses. The *Daybook* serves, in a way, like a portfolio. It is one simple form of portfolio assessment.

3. Can I photocopy these lessons?

No, unfortunately, you cannot. The selections, instruction, and activities are protected by copyright. To copy them infringes on the rights of the authors of the selections and the book. Writers such as Langston Hughes, Cynthia Rylant, and Ray Bradbury have granted permission for the use of their work in the *Daybooks* and to photocopy their work violates their copyright.

4. Can I skip around in the *Daybook*?

Yes, absolutely. The *Daybooks* were designed to allow teachers maximum flexibility. You can start with some of the later clusters (or units) and then pick up the earlier ones later on in the year. Or you can teach a lesson from here and one from there. But the optimum order of the book is laid out in the table of contents, and students will most likely see the logic and continuity of the book when they start at the beginning and proceed in order.

5. What is "annotating a text"? Are students supposed to write in the margin of the book?

Annotating refers to underlining parts of a text, circling words or phrases, highlighting with a colored marker, or taking notes in the margin. Students begin their school years marking up books in kindergarten and end, often in college, writing in the margins of their texts or highlighting key passages. Yet in the years in between—the majority of their school years—students are often forbidden from writing in their books, even though it represents a natural kinesthetic aid for memory and learning.

6. Why were these literature selections chosen?

The literature was chosen primarily for its high interest for students. Middle school teachers advised the editors how to construct a table of contents that had the selections with proven student appeal. The first, and foremost, criterion was the appeal of a selection for students.

But the literature was also carefully matched with the lesson concept. (A lesson on characters, for example, needed to present two or three strong characters for study.) So, in addition to high student appeal, the selections illustrate a specific aspect of critical reading and are representative of the diversity of our society.

7. What are the art and photos supposed to represent?

The art program for the *Daybooks* features the work of outstanding contemporary photographers. These photos open each unit and set the tone. Then, within each lesson, a number of smaller, somewhat enigmatic images are used. The purpose behind these images is not to illustrate what is happening in the literature or even to represent an interpretation of it. Rather, the hope is to stretch students' minds, hinting at connections, provoking the imagination, jarring loose a random thought or two about the selection. And, of course, the hope is that students will respond favorably to contemporary expressions of creativity.

8. In what way do the *Daybooks* teach critical thinking skills?

One of the hallmarks of the middle school *Daybooks* is their emphasis on critical thinking, such as predicting, inferencing, and evaluating. On the advice of practicing teachers, the middle school *Daybooks* purposely emphasized the key skills students need to improve their reading skills, such as finding the main idea, distinguishing fact from opinion, making inferences, reflecting on what you read, and so forth. In fact, critical thinking skills are taught across the grades, as the scope and sequence chart in this guide on pages 11–12 shows. The *Daybooks* are a marriage of strong teaching of critical reading skills with good literature and the consistent opportunity to write about what you read.

9. What are the boldface terms in the lesson all about?

The terms boldfaced in the lessons appear in the back of the *Daybook*. The glossary includes key literary terms that 1) are used in the *Daybook* lessons, and 2) students are likely to encounter in literature classes. The glossary is another resource for students to use in reading and reacting to the literature.

Skill Instruction	Grade 6	Grade 7	Grade 8
Comprehension			
author's perspective/viewpoint	✓	✓	✓
author's purpose	✓	✓	✓
bias	✓	✓	
cause and effect	✓	✓	
change pace	✓		
compare and contrast	✓	✓	✓
details	✓	✓	✓
draw conclusions		✓	✓
evaluate	✓	✓	✓
fact and opinion	✓	✓	✓
generalize		✓	✓
inference	✓	✓	✓
make connections to personal life	✓	✓	✓
predict	✓	✓	✓
reflect	✓	✓	✓
respond to literature	✓	✓	✓
sequence	✓		✓
summarize	✓		✓
thesis statement	✓	✓	✓
visualize		✓	✓
Literary Elements/Author's Craft			
alliteration	✓		✓
author's style	✓	✓	✓
characterization	✓	✓	✓
imagery	✓	✓	
irony	✓	✓	✓
metaphor	✓	✓	✓
mood	✓	✓	✓
onomatopoeia		✓	
personification	✓	✓	
plot	✓	✓	✓
point of view	✓	✓	✓
repetition, rhyme, rhythm	✓	✓	✓
sensory language	✓	✓	✓
setting	✓	✓	✓
simile	✓	✓	✓
symbolism		✓	✓
text structure	✓	✓	✓
theme	✓	✓	✓
tone	✓	✓	✓
word choice	✓	✓	✓

Skill Instruction	Grade 6	Grade 7	Grade 8
Study and Word Skills			
formulate questions	✓	✓	
highlight	✓	✓	✓
preview	✓		✓
take notes	✓	✓	✓
use context clues	✓		
use graphic sources	✓	✓	✓
use structural clues	✓	✓	✓

Like the *Write Source 2000* handbook, the *Daybooks* will appeal to certain teachers who need versatile, flexible materials and who place a premium on books with high student appeal. Some teachers, by nature, are more eclectic in their teaching approach, and others are more consistent and patterned. Some teachers place a premium on student interest and relevance more than on structured, predictable lessons. The *Daybooks*, like *Write Source 2000,* are directed at more eclectic teachers and classrooms.

The *Daybooks* are organized to allow maximum flexibility. You can pick an individual lesson or cluster of lessons in order to feature a certain author or literary selection. Or, you may want to concentrate on a particular area of critical reading. In either case, the *Daybooks*, like *Write Source 2000,* allow you to pick up the book and use it for days or weeks at a time, then leave it, perhaps to teach a novel or longer writing project, and then return to it again later in the semester. You, not the text, set the classroom agenda.

Another similarity between the *Daybooks* and the *Write Source 2000* handbook lies in the approach to writing. Both begin from the premise that writing is, first and foremost, a means of discovery. "Writing to learn" is the common expression for this idea. Only by expression can we discover what lies within us. *Write Source 2000* introduces this idea in its opening chapter, and the *Daybooks*, by promoting daily writing, give you the tool to make writing a consistent, regular feature of your classes.

But the *Daybooks* only start students on a daily course of reading and writing. Individual writing assignments are initiated but not carried through to final drafts. The purpose of writing in the *Daybooks* is mostly one of discovery, creative expression, clarification of ideas or interpretations, and idea generation. The *Daybooks* are intended to be starting points, places to ruminate and organize thoughts about literature, as opposed to offering definitive instructions about how to craft an essay or write a persuasive letter. That's where *Write Source 2000* comes in. It picks up where the *Daybooks* leave off, providing everything students need to create a polished essay or literary work.

The accompanying chart correlates writing assignments in the *Daybooks* to *Write Source 2000.*

Daybook Lesson	Writing Activity	*Write Source 2000,* ©1999 *Reference*
Angles of Literacy		
1. Becoming an Active Reader	write about a poem	196-197, 287
2. Connecting to the Story	write a caption	196-197, 288
3. Language and Craft	compare two poems	196-197, 287, 312
4. An Author's Perspective	write an introduction	63, 288
5. Focus on the Writer	write about an author	52, 161-166

Daybook Lesson	Writing Activity	*Write Source 2000,* ©1999 *Reference*
Essentials of Reading		
1. Making Predictions	write a news story	167-174
2. Between the Lines	write a paragraph	98-99, 287
3. The Main Idea	create a graphic organizer	56, 284
4. Evaluating What You Read	write a recommendation	115-122, 289
5. Reflecting on a Writer's Words	write a journal entry	105, 145-148, 196-197
Essentials of Story		
1. Where the Story Happens	describe a story's mood	175-181, 285, 343
2. What a Character	write a character sketch	188, 284
3. Who's Telling the Story?	retell an incident	129-136, 288
4. The Plot	summarize a story	213-216, 285
5. The Theme	write a journal entry	105, 145-148
Understanding Theme		
1. Finding the Theme	write about a story's theme	175, 287, 366-368, 344-345
2. Themes in Poems	answer questions about a poem	196-197, 284
3. Themes in Fables	rewrite a fable	129-136, 192, 288
4. The Main Message	analyze a story's theme	143, 176, 287
5. The Secondary Message	plan a story	47, 145-159
The Art of Language		
1. Simile	write a poem	138-140, 198-200
2. Metaphor	analyze a poem	138-140, 196-197, 287
3. Assonance, Consonance, and Alliteration	write a poem	198-200, 202-203
4. Setting the Mood	analyze a story's mood	175, 287, 343
5. Symbolism	explain a statement	140, 285
The Art of Argument		
1. Taking a Position	react to a thesis statement	289, 366-368
2. Reasons and Evidence	reflect on a main point	288, 366-368
3. The Other Side	express your views on an issue	118-122, 287
4. Facts and Opinions	write a paragraph	98-99, 287, 289, 292
5. Weighing an Argument	compose an argument	118-122, 288

Daybook Lesson	Writing Activity	*Write Source 2000,* ©1999 *Reference*
Focus on the Writer: Cynthia Rylant		
1. Characters in Perspective	examine author's perspective	175, 287
2. Perspective and Style	react to an author's style	175, 288, 366-368
3. Perspective and Theme	explore a poem's theme	196-197, 287
4. Perspective in Autobiography	make personal connections	366-368
5. Reflecting on Perspective	write a journal entry	47, 145-148, 366-368
The Reader's Response		
1. Factual Response	write a profile	161-166, 285, 292
2. Interpretive Response	write interpretive questions	196-197, 285, 366-368
3. Supporting Your Interpretation	write a paragraph	98-99, 289
4. Evaluative Response	evaluate a story	176-181, 289
5. Connecting to Your Life	respond to a story	175-181, 287, 366-368
Active Reading: Social Studies		
1. Highlighting	write a paragraph	98-99, 288, 320
2. Summing Up	design a quiz	285, 288, 374-380
3. Pulling It Together	analyze details	287, 320
4. Reading the Visuals	create a graphic	56, 287-288
5. Patterns of Organization	write a summary	56, 213-216, 320
Active Reading: Narrative Nonfiction		
1. Story *and* Facts	identify facts	284, 292
2. What's the Big Idea?	plan a nonfiction piece	46-52, 366-368
3. Details, Details	analyze details	287, 290
4. Inferencing	write a profile	287
5. Author's Purpose	examine author's purpose	287
Style and Structure		
1. Style Choices	compare authors' word choice	287, 313
2. More Style Choices	compare authors' styles	130-136, 287, 313
3. The Structure	examine a character	176, 287
4. Poetic Structure	analyze a poem's structure	196-197, 202-207, 287
5. Structure *and* Style	complete a chart	143, 287, 289

Daybook Lesson	Writing Activity	Write Source 2000, ©1999 Reference
Poetic Forms and Techniques		
1. Breaking the Rules	analyze a poem	196-197, 202-205, 287
2. Patterns of Sound	write a news article	129-136, 167-174
3. The Sonnet	discuss sonnet form	196-197, 204-205
4. Haiku	discuss haiku form	196-197, 204-205
5. Free Verse	discuss free verse	194-197, 204-205
Active Reading: Persuasive Writing		
1. Viewpoint	write diary entries	145-148
2. Tone	compare two speeches	313, 287
3. Word Choice	examine word choice	20, 22, 82, 136, 287
4. Personal Experience	write a memo	252-253, 366-368
5. Brainstorming	write a paragraph	98-99, 103, 116-122, 366-368
Focus on the Writer: Mark Twain		
1. Early Attempts at Humor	explore uses of humor	175-181, 287
2. Exaggeration	examine exaggeration	138, 287
3. The Art of Satire	analyze satire	143, 287
4. Humor in Character	reflect on a character	176, 287
5. A Man of Letters	analyze humor	285, 287, 289

Angles of Literacy

by Louann Reid

When we view something of potential value, such as a diamond or an antique vase, we often examine it from all sides. We hold it up and slowly turn it, looking first at the front, then the sides and back. Combining information from each perspective, we construct a fuller picture of the object and its worth. Similarly, we can examine a concept or idea from several angles, or perspectives, using a variety of approaches to understand a complex concept. Perhaps no concept in education is more complex—or more important—than literacy.

"Literacy" is frequently defined as the ability to read and write. But people also need to be able to read critically, write effectively, draw diagrams, collaborate with others, listen carefully, and understand complex instructions. In short, literacy means being able to do whatever is required to communicate effectively in a variety of situations. Angles of Literacy is the term we use in these *Daybooks* to identify five approaches to becoming literate.

THE FIVE ANGLES

The Angles of Literacy are major perspectives from which to examine a text. Strategies within each angle further define each one. Activities in the *Daybooks* provide students with multiple opportunities to become autonomous users of the strategies on other literature that they will encounter.

The angles are listed in an order that reflects the way that readers and writers first engage with the text. They are encouraged to move gradually from that initial engagement to a more evaluative or critical stance where they study the author's language and craft, life, and work. They critique the texts they read and consider what other critics have written. Moving from engagement through interpretation to evaluation is the process that Louise Rosenblatt and later reader-response critics advocate.

In our own work with middle school and secondary school students, we have repeatedly seen the value of encouraging students to read and write using all three stages—engagement, interpretation, evaluation. We also know that students sometimes begin at a different stage in the process—perhaps with interpretation rather than engagement. So, our five angles are not meant to be a hierarchy. Students may begin their engagement with the text using any angle and proceed in any order. Depending on the text and the context, readers might start with making personal connections to the stories in an essay. If the text is by an author that the students know well, they might naturally begin by comparing this work to the author's other works.

STRATEGIES

Strategies are plans or approaches to learning. By using some strategies over and over, students can learn to comprehend any text. The *Daybook* activities, such as annotating or visualizing a specific poem, story, or essay, provide students multiple opportunities to develop these strategies. From using this scaffolding students gradually become more independent readers and, ultimately, fully literate.

Because strategies are employed through activities, it may seem at first that they are the same thing. Yet, it is important to remember that a strategy is a purposeful plan. When, as readers, we select a strategy such as underlining key phrases, we have selected this action deliberately to help us differentiate between important information and unimportant information. We may use a double-entry log (an activity) to identify the metaphors in a poem. Our purpose in doing so is to understand figurative language (a strategy).

At the end of each lesson, the strategies are explicitly stated. In a sentence or two, the main point of the activity is noted. When students complete all 70 lessons in a daybook, they will have 70 statements of what they, as active readers, can do to read critically and write effectively.

Reflection is a vital component in helping students understand the use of strategies. After using a particular strategy, students need to step back and consider whether the strategy worked or did not work. They might think about how an approach or a strategy can change their understanding of what they read and write. Students might ask themselves a series of questions such as: What have I done? What have I learned? What would I do differently next time? How did the angle or strategy affect my understanding? What would I understand differently if I had changed the angle or the strategy?

ACTIVITIES

Each lesson in these *Daybooks* contains activities for students. From rereading to discussing with a partner to making a story chart, students learn how to become more critical readers and more effective writers. Many activities encourage students to write to learn. Other activities encourage students to increase their understanding of a text by visualizing it in a sketch or a graphic organizer. But, as much as possible, the *Daybooks* try to encourage students to make a creative written response with a poem, some dialogue, a character sketch, or some other creative assignment.

We have selected activities that work particularly well with the texts in the lesson and with the strategies we want students to develop. However, as you will see when you and your students use the *Daybooks*, there are several possible activities that could reinforce a particular strategy. You may want to have students try some of these activities, such as making a story chart or using a double-entry log, when they read other texts in class. This would also be another opportunity to have students ask themselves the reflective questions.

Angles of Literacy

Angle of Vision	Strategies	Selected Activities
Interacting with a Text	• underlining key phrases • writing questions or comments in the margin • noting word patterns and repetitions • circling unknown words • keeping track of the story or idea as it unfolds	• Write down initial impressions. • Reread. • Write a summary of the poem. • Generate two questions and one "certainty." Then, discuss the questions and statement in a small group.
Making Connections to the Stories within a Text	• paying attention to the stories being told • connecting the stories to one's own experience • speculating on the meaning or significance of incidents	• Make a story chart with three columns—incident in the poem, significance of the incident, related incident in my life. • Write a news story of events behind the story in the poem.

Shifting Perspectives	• examining the author's viewpoint
	• analyzing arguments
	• evaluating persuasive techniques
	• forming interpretations
	• comparing texts
		• Discuss with a partner or small group how you might read a poem differently if:
		  the speaker were female
		  you believe the speaker is a parent
		• Rewrite the text from a different point of view.

Studying the Language and Craft of a Text	• understanding figurative language • looking at the way the author uses words • modeling the style of other writers • studying various kinds of literature	• Use a double-entry log to identify metaphors and the qualities implied by the comparison. • Examine the title of the poem and its relationship to the text.
Focusing on the Writer's Life and Work	• reading what the author says about the writing • reading what others say • making inferences about the connections between an author's life and work • analyzing the writer's style • paying attention to repeated themes and topics in the work by one author	• Read about the poet's life. Then make an inference chart to record evidence from the poet's life, an inference, a comparison to the poem. • Write an evaluation of the poem. Then read what one or more critics have said about the poem or poet. Finally, write a short response, either agreeing or disagreeing with the critic. Support your ideas with textual evidence.

Responding to Literature Through Writing

by Ruth Vinz

We have found that students' encounters with literature are enriched when they write their way toward understanding. The writing activities in the *Daybooks* are intended to help students explore and organize their ideas and reactions during and after reading. We make use of the exploratory and clarifying roles of writing through various activities.

Exploratory assignments include those through which students question, analyze, annotate, connect, compare, personalize, emulate, map, or chart aspects in the literary selections. Generally these assignments aid students' developing interpretations and reactions to the subjects, themes, or literary devices in the literature they are reading. Other writing activities offer students the opportunity to clarify their understanding of what they've read. These assignments lead students to look at other perspectives, determine the significance of what they read, and prioritize, interpret, question, and reflect on initial impressions. Further, students are asked to create literature of their own as a way of applying the concepts they're learning. Writing to clarify also involves students in reflection, where they are asked to think about their reactions and working hypotheses. Taken together, the writing activities represent a series of strategies that students can apply to the complex task of reading literature.

The writing activities included in the *Daybooks* start students on the path toward understanding. We did not take it as the function of the writing activities in this book to lead students through the writing process toward final, finished drafts. Although examples of extensions are included here in the Teacher's Guide, the writing in the *Daybooks* introduces first draft assignments that may lead into more formal writing if you, as the teacher, so choose.

You will have your own ideas about assisting students with the writing activities or extending the writing beyond the *Daybooks*. We think it's important for you to remind students that the writing in which they engage is useful for their reading outside the *Daybooks*. For example, students may use various types of maps, charts, or diagrams introduced in the *Daybooks* when they read a novel. They may find that the response notes become a strategy they use regularly. Once exposed to imitation and modeling, students may find these useful tools for understanding an author's style, language, or structure. If your students develop a conscious awareness of the strategies behind the particular writing activities, they can apply these in other reading situations.

Writing assignments to explore and to clarify students' developing interpretations are incorporated in two types of activities, both of which are elaborated on below.

WRITING ABOUT LITERATURE

You will find activities in every cluster of lessons that call upon students to write about the literature they are reading. We developed these writing assignments to help facilitate, stimulate, support, and shape students' encounters with literature. We think the assignments have four purposes:

(1) to connect the literature to the students' personal experiences; (2) to re-examine the text for various purposes (language and craft, connections with other texts, shifting perspectives, developing interpretations); (3) to develop hypotheses, judgments, and critical interpretations; (4) to apply the idea behind the lesson to a new literary text or situation.

The types of writing we have used to fulfill these purposes are:

1. Response Notes

Students keep track of their initial responses to the literature by questioning, annotating, and marking up the text in various ways. The response notes are used to get students in the habit of recording what they are thinking while reading. Many times we circle back and ask them to build on what they have written with a particular focus or way of responding. In the response notes, students are encouraged to make personal connections, re-examine text, jot down ideas for their own writing, and monitor their changing responses.

2. Personal Narrative

Students write personal stories that connect or relate to what they have read. In some cases, the narratives tell the stories of students' prior reading experiences or how a literary selection relates to their life experiences. Other activities use personal narrative to apply and refine students' understanding of narrative principles.

3. Idea Fund

Students collect ideas for writing—catalogs, lists, charts, clusters, diagrams, double-entry logs, sketches, or maps. These forms of idea gathering are useful for analyzing particular literary selections and will aid the initial preparation for longer pieces of critical analysis.

4. Short Response

Students write summaries; paraphrase main themes or ideas; and compose paragraphs of description, exposition, explanation, evaluation, and interpretation.

5. Analysis

Students write short analyses that take them beyond summarizing the literary selection or their personal reactions to it. The analytic activities engage students in recognizing symbols and figures of speech and the links between events, characters, or images. Again, these short analytical responses are intended to prepare students for longer, critical interpretation that you, as a teacher, might assign.

6. Speculation

Students' speculations are encouraged by writing activities that engage them in predicting, inferring, and imagining. "What if . . .," "How might . . .," and "Imagine that . . ." are all ways in which students are invited to see further possibilities in the literature they read.

Students use writing to record and reflect on their reactions and interpretations. At times, students are asked to share their writing with others. Such sharing is another form of reflection through which students have an opportunity to "see again" their own work in the context of what others have produced.

The writing activities in the *Daybooks* will help students connect what they read with what they experience and with what they write, and also to make connections between the literary selections and literary techniques. The activities encourage students to experiment with a range of forms, choose a range of focuses, and reflect on what they have learned from these. We hope the writing serves to give students access to a kind of literary experience they can value and apply in their future reading.

WRITING LITERATURE

Within a literary work, readers find a writer's vision, but readers also co-create the vision along with the writer and learn from his or her craft. We've asked our students to write literature of their own as a way of responding to what they read. Through writing literature, students can explore facets of the original work or use the techniques of a variety of authors. Here are a number of the activities introduced in the *Daybooks*:

1. Take the role of writer

Students write imaginative reconstructions of gaps in a text by adding another episode, adding dialogue, rewriting the ending, adding a section before or after the original text, adding characters, or changing the setting. Such imaginative entries into the text require that students apply their knowledge of the original.

2. Imitation and Modeling

The idea of modeling and imitation is not new. Writers learn from other writers. The modeling activities are intended to help students "read like a writer." In these activities, students experiment with nuances of expression, syntactic and other structural principles, and apply their knowledge of literary devices (for example, *rhythm, imagery, metaphor*). One goal in educating students with literature is to make explicit what writers do. One way to achieve the goal is to provide models that illustrate various principles of construction.

3. Original Pieces

Students write poems, character sketches, monologues, dialogues, episodes, vignettes, and descriptions as a way to apply the knowledge about language and craft they are gaining through their reading.

4. Living Others' Perspectives

Writing from others' viewpoints encourages students to step beyond self to imagine other perspectives. Students write from a character's point of view, compose diary entries or letters, explain others' positions or opinions, and other reactions to a situation. These writing activities encourage students to explore the concerns of others and to project other perspectives through their writing.

The writing becomes a record of students' developing and changing ideas about literature. By the time students have finished all of the writing in this book, they will have used writing strategies that can assist them in all future reading.

Reading, Writing, and Assessment

by Fran Claggett

As teachers, we all cope with the complexities of assessing student performance. We must be careful readers of student work, attentive observers of student participation in various activities, and focused writers in responding to student work. We must understand the value of rewarding what students do well and encouraging them to improve. Above all, we need to make the criteria for assessment clear to students.

THE DAYBOOKS

The *Daybooks* provide visible accounts of many aspects of the reading process. Students record all the various permutations of active reading and writing. In the current view of most teachers and researchers, reading is a process of constructing meaning through transactions with a text. In this view, the individual reader assumes responsibility for interpreting a text guided not only by the language of the text but also by the associations, cultural experiences, and prior knowledge that the reader brings to the interpretive task. Meaning does not reside solely within the words on the page. Our view of reading emphasizes the role of the reader. Construction of meaning, rather than the gaining and displaying of knowledge should be the goal of reading instruction. This rule is reflected throughout the *Daybooks*, which guide students in how to read, respond to, interpret, and reflect on carefully selected works of literature.

Within these lessons, students interact with a text from five angles of literacy. The *Daybooks* make it possible for both students and teachers to track students' increasing sophistication in using the angles to make sense of their reading. Through the strategies presented in the lessons, students learn to express their understanding of a text. They will do such things as show their understanding of figurative language and the importance of form; write about how characters are developed and change; and demonstrate their understanding of how a piece of literature develops.

THE ROLE OF THE TEACHER

The teacher is critical to the *Daybook* agenda. Conceivably, a teacher could pass out the *Daybooks* and turn the students loose, but that would not result in the carefully guided reading and writing that is intended. Rather, the teachers are central to student success. Because of the format of the *Daybooks*, lessons are short, each taking no more than a normal class period. They are intended to be complete in themselves, yet most teachers will see that there are numerous opportunities for extensions, elaborations, further readings, group work, and writing. The Teacher's Guide provides some suggestions; you will think of many others. The *Daybooks* offer guidelines for reading and thinking, for writing and drawing used in the service of reading. They also provide many opportunities for students to write pieces of their own, modeling, responding, interpreting, and reflecting on the pieces that they have read. Many of these pieces might lead to later revision, refining, group response, and editing. It is the teacher, however, who knows the students well enough to see which pieces would be worthwhile to work with and which it is best to leave as exercises rather than completed works.

In assessing the *Daybooks*, it is important to remember to look at the students' growing facility with the processes of reading. As is true with all learning, there will be false starts, abandoned practices, and frustrations, yet also illuminations, progress, and occasional epiphanies. No music teacher ever graded every attempt at mastering a piece of music. We, too, must resist the urge—honed by years of assessing only products or finished papers—of overassessing the *Daybooks*. We must consider them the place where students are free to think things through, change their minds, even start over. But you can be alert to what the student is doing well, what is frustrating, what needs more time. To that end, we have provided a chart which may be useful in getting a sense of how students are progressing in using angles of literacy. By duplicating the chart for each student, you can track progress through the lessons. We would like to encourage the idea of jotting down notations as you work with students during the class period or look over the *Daybooks* after class. In this way, you can amass a sizable amount of information over a grading period. Coupled with a student self-assessment, you will have tangible evidence of achievement in the *Daybooks*.

INDIVIDUAL STUDENT EIGHT-WEEK ASSESSMENT CHART

The columns for each week's lessons can be used in different ways. We suggest the number system: a 5 for insightful, imaginative thinking or responding, a 1 for a minimal attempt. Some teachers prefer the check, check-plus, check-minus system. There is even room, if you turn the chart sideways, to make some notations.

Angles of Literacy

INTERACTING WITH A TEXT	I	II	III	IV	V	VI	VII	VIII
The student demonstrates understanding by using interactive strategies such as:								
underlining key phrases								
writing questions or comments in the margin								
noting word patterns and repetitions								
circling unknown words								
keeping track of ideas as they unfold								

MAKING CONNECTIONS	I	II	III	IV	V	VI	VII	VIII
The student makes connections to the stories in a text by:								
paying attention to the stories in the text								
connecting ideas and themes in the text to personal ideas, experience, feelings, and knowledge								
making connections to other texts, movies, television shows, or other media								

SHIFTING PERSPECTIVES	I	II	III	IV	V	VI	VII	VIII
The student is able to shift perspectives to examine a text from many angles. When prompted, the student will engage in such strategies as:								
examining the author's viewpoint								
analyzing arguments								
evaluating persuasive techniques								
comparing texts								

STUDYING THE LANGUAGE AND CRAFT OF A TEXT

	I	II	III	IV	V	VI	VII	VIII

The student will demonstrate an understanding of the way language and craft operate in a text. Specifically, the student will:

show how imagery, metaphor, and figurative language are central to literature

demonstrate an understanding of how an author's vocabulary and use of language are integral to the overall work

use modeling to demonstrate an understanding of style and form

demonstrate understanding of various genres and forms of literature

FOCUSING ON THE WRITER

	I	II	III	IV	V	VI	VII	VIII

The student will demonstrate a rich understanding of a single writer's work, including:

interpreting short texts by the author

making inferences about the connections between an author's life and work

analyzing the writer's style

drawing conclusions about repeated themes and topics in an author's work

evaluating a text or comparing works by the same author

Unit Overview

This unit provides students with tools of active reading. Each lesson shows students how to connect to the poetry and nonfiction of Langston Hughes in a variety of methods: by studying his word choice and patterns, his topics, his use of language, his perspective, and his background.

Literature Focus

	Lesson	Literature
1.	Becoming an Active Reader	**Langston Hughes,** "Alabama Earth" / "Theme for English B" (Poetry)
2.	Connecting to the Story	**Langston Hughes,** "Aunt Sue's Stories" (Poetry)
3.	Language and Craft	**Langston Hughes,** "The Weary Blues" (Poetry)
4.	An Author's Perspective	**Langston Hughes,** from *The Return of Simple* (Nonfiction)
5.	Focus on the Writer	**Langston Hughes,** from *I Wonder As I Wander* (Autobiography)

Reading Focus

1. As an active reader, jot down notes, mark up the text, and ask questions. This helps you better understand and respond to a work of literature.
2. Comparing your own experiences to the events in a piece of literature helps you become more involved with the text.
3. Pay special attention to a writer's word choice and the way that words are arranged. This will help you understand what the writer is trying to convey about a subject.
4. Understanding an author's perspective helps you figure out what the author is trying to "tell" you in a piece of writing.
5. Keeping in mind what you know about an author will help you connect the writer and his or her work.

Writing Focus

1. Write a summary of a discussion about a poem.
2. Write a caption for a character's photo in a family album.
3. Analyze how Hughes changes language as his topic and purpose change.
4. Write an introduction to an anthology of Hughes's writing.
5. Create an introduction for a speech honoring Langston Hughes.

One Becoming an Active Reader

C r i t i c a l   R e a d i n g

FOCUS

Annotating a text helps a reader understand a piece of literature.

BACKGROUND

James Mercer Langston Hughes (1902-1967) has been called possibly the most influential African American writer of the twentieth century. His careers included poet, journalist, playwright, and lecturer. Hughes was the first black American to support himself entirely by writing and giving lectures. After a turbulent childhood, at twenty-one Hughes enrolled in Columbia University, the setting for the lesson's poem. However, he remained there for only one year. Students may be interested to know, as they read this poem with an academic setting, that Hughes left the university because of the bigotry and indifference that he found there.

➤ This lesson introduces students to the tools of active reading. Students interact with the text by writing notes, questions, reactions, and key ideas as they read. Stress to students that reading is not passive; it is active, requiring engagement to fully comprehend new text.

FOR DISCUSSION AND REFLECTION

➤ What questions do you have about "Theme for English B"? (Responses will vary.)

➤ What do you learn about the speaker's life through his poem? (Answers may include that he was twenty-two, was born in Winston-Salem, went to school in Durham, was the only black in his class, lived in the Harlem Branch Y, and so on.)

➤ What is "true" that came out of the page of assigned writing? (Responses will vary. The speaker presents the case that although black, he is like all of the others in his class and like the instructor: "I guess being colored doesn't make me *not* like / the same things other folks like who are other races." The speaker also points out the sameness of all people: "You are white— / yet a part of me, as I am a part of you. / That's American.")

W r i t i n g

QUICK ASSESS

Do students' summaries:

✓ include a variety of responses to the poem?

✓ reflect a thoughtful reading of the poem?

✓ comment on the value of the response notes?

Students should review their response notes for "Theme for English B" and share these in pairs. Using their notes, they will write a summary of what they learned in the discussion.

READING AND WRITING EXTENSIONS

➤ Invite students to draw a map of the speaker's route from school to home based on the stanzas from "Theme for English B." You might bring in a map of Harlem to check the maps' accuracy.

➤ Have students work in groups to investigate other black poets of the Harlem Renaissance—Claude McKay, Countee Cullen, Zora Neale Hurston, Rudolph Fisher, James Weldon Johnson, and Jean Toomer. Have each group make a poster to present selected interesting facts.

See also Answer Key, page 111

Two Connecting to the Story

Critical Reading

FOCUS

Active readers know how to make personal connections to the stories they read:

"He knows that Aunt Sue never got her stories / Out of any book at all, / But that they came / Right out of her own life."

BACKGROUND

Lesson Two shows that readers connect to literature when they can associate it with prior knowledge or a personal experience in their background. While the students' backgrounds may be distinctly different from that of Langston Hughes, many young readers will be able to relate to the speaker of the poem, someone remembering a relative who had a whole "head full of stories."

➤ Students might remember a movie, documentary, or text that taught them about slavery ("Black slaves / Working in the hot sun"), or they might connect to the mood of comfort and intimacy between an aunt and nephew on summer evenings on the front porch.

FOR DISCUSSION AND REFLECTION

➤ Describe the mood of the poem. (Answers may include secure, quiet, pensive, intimate.)

➤ What are the "dark shadows that cross and recross / Aunt Sue's stories"? (Students' responses will vary. Literally, the shadows may refer to the shadows visible on those summer nights. They may also represent the slaves or other black people whom Aunt Sue talks about.)

➤ What personal connections do you make with the poem? (Answers will vary, but you might get students thinking by sharing experiences or people that the poem reminds you of.)

➤ Who do you know that has a head and a heart "full of stories"? (Responses will vary but could include relatives, friends, teachers, favorite authors, and so on.)

Writing

QUICK ASSESS

Do students' captions:

✓ show the mood of the poem?

✓ explain Aunt Sue's importance in the family?

Because the poem paints such a detailed vignette, students are asked to imagine that they are part of Aunt Sue's family. Brainstorm what Aunt Sue might look like. Then have students compose a caption for a photograph of Aunt Sue, expressing why she is so important to the family and to them personally.

READING AND WRITING EXTENSIONS

➤ Encourage students to use their artistic talents to visualize details of Aunt Sue's stories through a sketch, watercolor, or clay model.

➤ Suggest that students preserve their own family history by asking an older family member to tell them a story. Students may want to record it in prose or poetry. Encourage students to share their stories with classmates.

Three Language and Craft

Critical Reading

FOCUS

In "The Weary Blues," Langston Hughes uses conversational language:

"He played that sad raggy tune like a musical fool. / Sweet Blues!"

BACKGROUND

David Littlejohn critiqued the work of Langston Hughes by describing the rhythm of his writing: "By molding his verse always on the sound of Negro talk, the rhythms of Negro music, by retaining his own keen honesty and directness, his poetic sense and ironic intelligence; he maintained through four decades a readable newness distinctly his own."

➤ "The Weary Blues" provides another rich example of Hughes's use of rhythm and language. In this poem, the upbeat mood comes from the sound words, repetition, and line breaks. It resembles the music for which it is named.

➤ Students may appreciate a little background on Blues music, a genre of African American folk and popular song. You may want to bring in recordings by Ma Rainey, Bessie Smith, B. B. King, or Ray Charles. Blues lyrics often deal with the hardships of life and love, a topic in Hughes's poem, and they are typically arranged in stanzas that include the repetition of certain lines: "Ain't got nobody in all this world, / Ain't got nobody but ma self."

FOR DISCUSSION AND REFLECTION

➤ What description do you find particularly striking? (Answers will vary.)

➤ What musical terms are used to show the connection of the poem to music? (Answers may include "syncopated tune," "ivory key," "raggy tune," or "deep song voice.")

➤ Have students compare the word choice, figurative language, style, and sound devices of "Theme for English B" to those of "The Weary Blues." (Many responses are possible but push students to offer specific text support for their views.)

Writing

QUICK ASSESS

Do students' charts:

✓ show differences between the two poems?

✓ reflect thoughtful readings of both poems?

It might help students to analyze Hughes's craft—word choice, style, sound devices, and figurative language—if you break the class into four groups, with each analyzing one element. Have each group share its findings and complete the chart on the board.

READING AND WRITING EXTENSIONS

➤ Encourage students to rewrite "The Weary Blues" in the more formal style of "Theme for English B." Suggest that students remove slang, end rhyme, and the AAB pattern, and invite them to read their new versions.

➤ Ask students to write a poem about how they feel when they listen to one of their favorite songs. Encourage them to use figurative language and sound devices to express their mood.

See also Answer Key, page 111

Four An Author's Perspective

Critical Reading

FOCUS

In *Newsweek*, Saul Maloff described Langston Hughes's character Jesse B. Simple as a "hilarious black Socrates of the neighborhood saloons."

BACKGROUND

In this lesson, students turn to Langston Hughes's work as a journalist. In 1943, Hughes began working for the *Chicago Defender* as a newspaper columnist and developed a feature around one character, Jesse B. Simple. Simple is a poor resident of Harlem, a kind of comic no-good, a stereotype Hughes turned to advantage. In the column, Simple tells stories to Boyd, a writer, in exchange for drinks.

➤ At times, Hughes used Simple as a mouthpiece of his own views. For example, he laments being a minority not represented in history books, criticizing those "who make up the most . . . then write the history books and leave *us* out, or else put in the books nothing but prize fighters and ballplayers."

FOR DISCUSSION AND REFLECTION

➤ What notable African Americans does Hughes mention in this one column? (Answers include Jackie Robinson, W. E. B. Du Bois, Booker T. Washington, Frederick Douglass, Gabriel and Nat Turner, Denmark Vesey, and African kings such as Ashanti and Benin.)

➤ Does Simple think black history is taught the same in the North as in the South? (No. He says that southern "teachers teach children about *our* history. It is not like up North where almost no teachers teach children anything about themselves and who they is and where they come from . . . .")

➤ What do you learn about Hughes's perspective toward African American history from what Simple and Boyd say? (Answers may include that textbook history does a disservice to African Americans since most of their experiences are left out.)

Writing

QUICK ASSESS

Do students' introductions:

✓ comment on Hughes's life, perspective, and purposes?

✓ use information from a variety of texts?

Before students develop an introduction to an anthology of work by Langston Hughes, have them page through all of the lessons of the unit, reflecting on the kinds of writing they have read and the different purposes Hughes had for his poetry and prose.

READING AND WRITING EXTENSIONS

➤ Encourage students to read from Jackie Robinson's autobiography, *I Never Had It Made*, to understand the reference Simple uses in the newspaper column.

➤ Have students think about what other experiences, events, or figures some people might think have been left out of many history books. Invite them to share their ideas with their classmates.

See also Answer Key, page 111

Five Focus on the Writer

Critical Reading

FOCUS

Langston Hughes on his hopes for the future:

"I began to puzzle out how I, a *Negro*, could make a living in America from writing."

BACKGROUND

Langston Hughes wrote two autobiographies. In his first, *The Sea*, he struggled with his identity in America: "You see, I am not black. There are lots of different kinds of blood in our family. But here in the United States, the word Negro is used to mean anyone who has any Negro blood at all in his veins. In Africa, the word is more pure. It means all Negro, therefore black." In his second autobiography, *I Wonder As I Wander*, the focus of this lesson, Hughes continues to struggle with issues of identity.

➤ Lesson Five asks students to read an excerpt from *I Wonder As I Wander* and make connections between Hughes's life and his writings. Remind students that while everything that Hughes writes is not directly about his life, they should be able to make a number of connections between his life and the works included in this unit.

FOR DISCUSSION AND REFLECTION

➤ From what you have read, do you believe Hughes eventually reached a point where he could "write seriously . . . about the Negro people"? (Answers may include that his poems reflect their culture of music, the pain of slavery, their close ties with family. His prose presents African American historical figures and the ignorance of white people about black history.)

➤ What kind of writing did Hughes not want to do? (Responses may vary, but students should mention the fake true stories and commercially successful short stories Hughes criticizes in this excerpt.)

Writing

QUICK ASSESS

Do students' introductions:

✔ cover the topics of Hughes's early writing, his obstacles, and his messages?

✔ explain why he is worthy of an award?

By reviewing the poetry and prose in the unit, students will create a timeline of four or five major events of Hughes's life. With all of this information in mind, students will be prepared to write an introductory speech for an awards ceremony honoring Langston Hughes.

READING AND WRITING EXTENSIONS

➤ Invite students to read several selections from the unit on Cynthia Rylant (pp. 103–116). Have them compare and contrast how the two writers, Rylant and Hughes, reveal their perspective through their writing.

➤ Have students think about Hughes's statement that he "had better go sit in the sun awhile and think, having just been through a tense and disheartening winter . . . ." Then ask students to imagine that they are Hughes and to write a letter to a good friend about the source of his frustration and unhappiness.

See also Answer Key, page 111

Unit Overview

The five lessons of this unit focus on the reading strategies of predicting outcomes, making inferences, determining the main idea, evaluating writing, and reflecting after reading. Students will develop and practice these skills as they read poetry by Eve Merriam, autobiography by Maya Angelou, and a nonfiction piece by Walter Dean Myers.

Literature Focus

	Lesson	Literature
1.	Making Predictions	**Maya Angelou,** from *I Know Why the Caged Bird Sings* (Autobiography)
2.	Between the Lines	**Maya Angelou,** from *I Know Why the Caged Bird Sings* (Autobiography)
3.	The Main Idea	**Walter Dean Myers,** from *Now Is Your Time!* (Nonfiction-Social Studies)
4.	Evaluating What You Read	
5.	Reflecting on a Writer's Words	**Eve Merriam,** "Like Bookends" (Poetry)

Reading Focus

1. As you read, look for clues that point to what will happen next. Base your predictions on details in the text to be sure that your predictions make sense.
2. Look for details in the text that help you make inferences about characters and events.
3. The main idea is the point that a writer wants to make. As you read, look for details that will help you determine what the writer wants you to think about the topic.
4. Evaluating a piece of writing helps you form an opinion and gives you a better understanding of the piece.
5. Reflecting on a piece of writing and connecting it to your own experiences helps you figure out what it means to you.

Writing Focus

1. Use predictions about what will happen next in a story to write an article about an event for a school newspaper.
2. Make inferences about an author's feelings.
3. Create a graphic organizer to show the relationship between main idea and supporting details.
4. Recommend one of two books to a classmate.
5. Write a journal entry connecting a poem to personal experiences.

One Making Predictions

Critical Reading

BACKGROUND

This lesson is designed to help students understand why making predictions is a valuable strategy of active readers. By interacting with the text and making educated guesses on what might follow, readers become involved in the story. The excerpt from *I Know Why the Caged Bird Sings* has been divided at points where readers can make such predictions. To help them make sensible guesses, advise students to go back to the text to find details that give a hint about a possible outcome.

➤ Maya Angelou is a prolific African American writer, having worked as an essayist, playwright, poet, editor, and screenplay writer. Her early life was tumultuous. Born Marguerite Johnson, in 1928, in St. Louis, Missouri, Angelou (her later stage name) was raised in the South by her grandmother, "Momma," after her parents divorced. At the age of seven, she was raped by her mother's boyfriend (who was later murdered by her uncles). As a result of trauma from the rape, Angelou became mute for five years. She was persuaded to speak by an educated black woman, Mrs. Flowers. According to Angelou, Mrs. Flowers, "emphasized the importance of the spoken word, explained the nature of and importance of education, and instilled in her a love of poetry." Mrs. Flowers also persuaded her to return to school. At Angelou's eighth grade graduation, which is the topic of the excerpt in this lesson, she ranked at the top in her class at Lafayette County Training School in Stamps, Arkansas.

FOR DISCUSSION AND REFLECTION

➤ How is the mood created in the first part of the excerpt? (The mood is cheerful and exciting. Angelou says "I hoped the memory of that morning would never leave me," God had "allowed me to live to see this day," and "It was a dream of a day.")

➤ What details mark a dramatic change in mood in the second part of the excerpt? (Answers may include that the school now "seemed cold and unfriendly," that a "sense of ill-fated timing crept over" Angelou, and that she "was overcome with a presentiment of worse things to come.")

Writing

Write the predictions for the last excerpt on the board. Ask students to support their predictions for something good, bad, surprising, and so on with text details that support each prediction. Then students will choose one of the outcomes and write a news article for the Lafayette School newspaper about the graduation.

READING AND WRITING EXTENSIONS

➤ Have students reflect on how Angelou felt when she opened Bailey's gift, the collection of Edgar Allan Poe poems. Encourage them to write about a time when they received a special gift.

➤ Invite students to read "On the Pulse of Morning," Angelou's poem for the inauguration of President Clinton on January 20, 1993. Have them discuss how the poem demonstrates the poet's gift for survival in the face of hardship and injustice.

Two Between the Lines

Critical Reading

FOCUS

Robert A. Gross of *Newsweek,* on Maya Angelou's autobiography:

"Miss Angelou's book is more than a tour de force of language or the story of childhood suffering; it quietly and gracefully portrays and pays tribute to the courage, dignity and endurance of the small, rural community in which she spent most of her early years."

BACKGROUND

In "Between the Lines," students should look for the meaning beyond the written word. It will be easy for students to understand Angelou's negative feelings about the guest speaker, but you may need to encourage them to "read between the lines" to infer what she was feeling about her education. For example, Angelou's thoughts about the valedictorian's speech, "To Be or Not to Be," ("Hadn't he heard the whitefolks? We couldn't *be,* so the question was a waste of time") allow us to conclude that she senses that all of her hard work was worthless. When Angelou writes, "I marveled that Henry could go through with the speech as if we had a choice," readers can infer that she feels defeated and hopeless.

FOR DISCUSSION AND REFLECTION

➤ How does Angelou feel about her graduation honors? (Answers may include disappointed, worthless, and inferior to the whites in the nearby all-white school.)

➤ How does Angelou's mood change? (Students should recognize the pride that Angelou comes to feel. Responses may focus on her realization of the meaning of the Negro National Anthem, the leadership of the valedictorian, the response of the audience, and so on.)

➤ Ask students to describe a time when they for the first time saw meaning and personal significance in the words of a speech, song, poem, or famous saying—as Angelou did with the words to "Jesus Loves Me This I Know."

Writing

QUICK ASSESS

Do students' paragraphs:

✓ reflect appropriate inferences?

✓ include supporting evidence from the autobiography?

Working in pairs, students should "tell back" the story of Maya Angelou's graduation day from start to finish before creating a web to describe the meaning of her graduation. Then students will be prepared to write a paragraph about Angelou's feelings based on their inferences.

READING AND WRITING EXTENSIONS

➤ Invite students to imagine they are Henry Reed. Have them write a journal entry about what happened at the graduation from his point of view.

➤ Encourage students to read from *The Complete Collected Poems of Maya Angelou* and to write a reader's response to the imagery of one poem they enjoy.

Three The Main Idea

Critical Reading

FOCUS

The writer of nonfiction organizes his or her material to convey a main idea.

BACKGROUND

Lesson Three presents students with an excerpt from a nonfiction piece about the 1954 *Brown vs. Board of Education of Topeka* court case. This landmark ruling led to the desegregation of schools and almost four decades of busing to equalize school populations. The author, Walter Dean Myers (1937–), is probably best known for his fiction about teenagers facing the obstacles of inner-city life.

➤ The main point of the trial was that if segregation were declared unconstitutional in the schools, then all segregation "could be declared unconstitutional." At the trial, an African American psychologist, Dr. Kenneth B. Clark, demonstrated that a lifetime of segregation was harmful to black children. According to Myers, Clark "showed that black children felt inferior to white children." The Justice Department argued that "racial segregation was objectionable . . . and hurt our relationships with other nations." As a result of this case, the Supreme Court passed a ruling giving equality in education to blacks by banning segregation.

FOR DISCUSSION AND REFLECTION

➤ Summarize Dr. Kenneth B. Clark's testimony in the case. (He showed that black children felt that black colored dolls were inferior just based on color. He felt segregation led to this feeling of inferiority and that a sense of inferiority caused black children to perform poorly.)

➤ Why was this victory different from others achieved by blacks? (Answers might include that it was not an escape from slavery, not a victory on a battlefield, not a victory through writing, but a legal victory.)

Writing

QUICK ASSESS

Do students' graphic organizers:

✔ express Myers's main idea clearly?

✔ show the relationship between the main idea and supporting details?

As students consider the relationship between main idea and details, provide them with the visual structures for various graphic organizers—a traditional outline, a flowchart, a ladder, a timeline. Ask them to work in small groups to use one of the organizers and share their structures with each other.

READING AND WRITING EXTENSIONS

➤ Encourage students to read excerpts from one of Walter Dean Myers's novels of black teenagers living in Harlem—*The Young Landlords, Motown and Didi, Scorpions,* or *The Mouse Rap.* Have them share their impressions.

➤ Suggest that students do more research on the topic of segregation in schools or on other racial and ethnic issues that continue today. Invite them to discuss their findings with the class.

See also Answer Key, page 112

Four Evaluating What You Read

Critical Reading

FOCUS

Readers need to understand why they like or dislike a selection.

BACKGROUND

In this lesson, students are asked to develop criteria for evaluating the passage by Walter Dean Myers that they read in Lesson Three. You may want to help them brainstorm a list of criteria that they could use to decide the quality of a piece of writing before they try to judge the specific work. Although they are familiar with evaluating—rating movies, CDs, TV shows, consumer products, and so on—they may find it difficult to identify specific criteria on which their judgments are made.

➤ Help students see that evaluating is an essential reading skill. Glenna Sloan writes: "Genuine criticism is a systematic study that treats literature as an art. It involves talking about literature . . . taking the student beyond the subjectivity of his experience out into a wider, more comprehensive world."

FOR DISCUSSION AND REFLECTION

➤ What makes you like a piece of writing? (Responses will vary, but you should encourage students to examine the criteria on which their opinions rest.)

➤ Does narrative or nonfiction draw a reader closer to an idea? (Answers will vary.)

➤ Would the gender or age of a protagonist influence how much you like a piece of writing? (Students' answers will vary but should include specific works and characters.)

Writing

QUICK ASSESS

Do students' recommendations:

✔ make a clear case for one of the readings?

✔ present reasons to support the argument?

Students are asked to write a book recommendation for either *Now Is Your Time!* or *I Know Why the Caged Bird Sings* based on specific criteria. Their recommendations may be structured in three parts: a thesis sentence, which recommends one of the books; a body, which includes specific reasons; and a conclusion, which describes their personal responses to their chosen book.

READING AND WRITING EXTENSIONS

➤ Encourage students to read about the criteria for some of the famous awards— Newbery, Caldecott, Edgar Allan Poe, Coretta Scott King, and so on—that many of the books they read have won.

➤ Ask students to list five books (all of one kind, such as mystery or science fiction or fantasy) that they have read and enjoyed. Then have them list the qualities all five of those works share. Invite them to discuss their lists with classmates and try to agree on a list of criteria with which a "good" fantasy, mystery, or science fiction book could be chosen.

Five Reflecting on a Writer's Words

Critical Reading

FOCUS

By reflecting on what they read, active readers can figure out what a piece of writing means to them.

BACKGROUND

Eve Merriam (1916—1992) has done it all in the field of writing—poetry, novels, plays, and picture books for both children and adults. "Like Bookends" focuses on the erratic relationship between an adolescent and his parents, a relationship that can change with the mood swings of the teen.

➤ This lesson looks at another reading strategy active readers should use, connecting to a piece by determining how the work affects them personally. A personal connection is really a reflection after reading, an attempt to figure out what meaning, if any, the work has for the reader. Give students cues—"This reminds me of the time . . . ." or "I remember . . . ."—to help them connect to lines within "Like Bookends."

FOR DISCUSSION AND REFLECTION

➤ Describe the relationship between the speaker and his parents. (It is strained, distant, and awkward. The parents are "unable to read" the child's feelings, and the conversation is stale and boring: "How was your day dear / *Fine.*")

➤ How does the imagery of the napkins reflect the change in mood at the table? (First, the napkins are politely folded, showing the tension. Then the napkins swirl away with spontaneous conversation. Next, the napkins become parachutes that bring the family back to restraint again.)

➤ Is this poem "good"? (Answers to this question will probably vary but encourage students to cite specific criteria for their judgments.)

Writing

QUICK ASSESS

Do students' journal entries:

✓ offer a personal connection to the poem?

✓ express their feelings about the family in the poem?

Before students write a personal journal entry about the poem, it might help to have them share their responses to the poem in small groups. If some students seem to have trouble making personal connections, ask for a volunteer to read his or her entry to the class.

READING AND WRITING EXTENSIONS

➤ Invite students to think of a simile to express the relationship between their parents (or older relatives) and them. Merriam uses bookends but help them to think of something different. Then ask students to write a poem, using "Like Bookends" as a model, that extends their similes.

➤ Invite students to draw or sketch a picture that could be used to illustrate Merriam's poem. Display the drawings for all to see, discuss, and enjoy.

Unit Overview

This unit focuses on the essential elements of a story: setting, character, point of view, plot, and theme. As students read and respond to excerpts from novels by Yoshiko Uchida and Elizabeth George Speare and a short story by Judith Gorog, they will learn how to recognize a well-constructed story and to appreciate the choices writers make in crafting their works.

Literature Focus

	Lesson	Literature
1.	Where the Story Happens	**Yoshiko Uchida,** from *Journey to Topaz* (Fiction)
2.	What a Character	**Elizabeth George Speare,** from *The Witch of Blackbird Pond* (Fiction)
3.	Who's Telling the Story?	
4.	The Plot	**Judith Gorog,** "Those Three Wishes" (Short Story)
5.	The Theme	

Reading Focus

1. Details included in the description of the setting help convey a particular mood or feeling in a story.

2. Look for clues to a character's personality from the actions, thoughts, and dialogue of the character, and the reactions of other characters.

3. Determine the point of view of a story. It will help you figure out whether the information you are getting about characters and events is from a limited or omniscient perspective.

4. As you read a story, take time to examine the main events of the plot. This will help you see the relationships between events of the story.

5. The theme is the underlying meaning or lesson about life in a story. As you read a story, decide how the story's meaning relates to you.

Writing Focus

1. Describe the mood of a piece based on the author's choice of images.

2. Write a brief character sketch.

3. Write about an incident by using a different point of view than the author did.

4. Write a summary of a story's plot.

5. Compose a journal entry about a personal experience that relates to the story's theme.

One Where the Story Happens

Critical Reading

FOCUS

The description of the setting helps to convey a story's mood:

"Yuki thought she had never seen a more dreary place in all her life. There wasn't a single tree or a blade of grass to break the monotony of the sun-bleached desert."

BACKGROUND

The mood, or atmosphere, in a story is often created by its setting and characterization. Lesson One focuses on the sensory details that an author uses to describe a setting and to establish the mood.

➤ In *Journey to Topaz*, Yoshiko Uchida offers a detailed description of the forbidding area around a Japanese internment camp in Topaz, Utah, a desolate place located in the middle of the Great Basin. In this excerpt, eleven-year-old Yuki Sakane first arrives at Topaz, the concentration camp she will live in for four years.

➤ Students may appreciate a little background about Yoshiko Uchida. Born in California, the daughter of two Japanese immigrants, Uchida and her family were moved to Topaz in 1942. During World War II, more than 120,000 West Coast Japanese Americans were uprooted to similar government detention camps, for no other reason than their Japanese ancestry. Many of Uchida's writings deal with the experiences of Japanese Americans before, during, and after World War II.

FOR DISCUSSION AND REFLECTION

➤ How does Uchida establish the mood? (Responses will vary but may include similes such as the powdery desert dust engulfing her "like a smothering blanket," the Boy Scouts looking "like flour-dusted cookies that had escaped from a bakery," or the landscape appearing "like the carcass of a chicken stripped clean of any meat and left all dry, brittle bone.")

➤ What effective sensory images does Uchida use? (Sight images include tall mountains, sheltering shadows, and "squat tar-papered barracks sitting in a pool of white dust." Touch images include a smothering blanket, a new road still soft with churned up dust, and the blazing sun, which made Yuki "feel dry and parched deep down inside.")

Writing

QUICK ASSESS

Do students' descriptions:

✔ focus on the mood created by the setting?

✔ include evidence from the selection?

Pair students to share their images of sight and touch from the selection and then have them brainstorm words that might describe mood: lighthearted, angry, cozy, hopeful, tense, despairing, fearful, and so on. Then students will describe how Uchida's images contribute to the overall mood created by the setting.

READING AND WRITING EXTENSIONS

➤ Invite students to read *Baseball Saved Us*, a picture book by Ken Mochizuki, which explains how a Japanese American boy learns baseball when he and his family are forced to live in an internment camp during World War II. Have students discuss the setting.

➤ Suggest that students read from *I'm in Charge of Celebrations*, a picture book by Byrd Baylor. Have them explain how its mood compares or contrasts to the mood of *Journey to Topaz*.

See also Answer Key, page 112

Two What a Character

Critical Reading

FOCUS
Elizabeth George Speare is known for "creating believable characters who rely on their inner strength to cope with the challenges they face."

BACKGROUND

This lesson focuses on the techniques that an author uses to create a memorable character. Remind students that characterization, or the development of a fictional character, is not always direct. Readers often need to make inferences about a character's personality by piecing together what the character says, thinks, and does and analyzing the reactions of other characters.

➤ Elizabeth George Speare created a memorable character in Barbados-born Kit Tyler, who travels to Connecticut, befriends a Quaker woman, and is later accused of being a witch. Speare presents Kit in a variety of ways. Students can see her headstrong nature through her words ("'Turn back, Captain,' she ordered impulsively"), her looks ("Kicking off her buckled shoes and dropping the woolen cloak"), her actions ("she plunged headlong over the side of the boat"), her thoughts (about how "her grandfather cautioned her to think before she flew off the handle"), and the reactions of others ("Then she saw that the child . . . was staring at her with a gaze of pure worship").

FOR DISCUSSION AND REFLECTION

➤ Which of Kit's actions are met with disapproval? (Answers may include her ordering the captain, jumping overboard, ruining her clothing, and knowing how to swim.)

➤ What feelings does Kit reveal? (Answers may include that she is regretful for the trip up north, grateful for the return, angry when she is ignored, amused when she passes Nathaniel in the water, indignant when she is criticized about her clothes, and so on.)

➤ Does Kit remind you of anyone you know? (Responses will vary.)

Writing

QUICK ASSESS
Do students' character sketches:
✔ use evidence from the excerpt?
✔ reveal Kit's personality?

Using the information from their trait charts, students will write a character sketch of Kit Tyler, describing her for someone who has never read the story.

READING AND WRITING EXTENSIONS

➤ Encourage students to read from one of Speare's other historical fiction books—*Calico Captive, The Bronze Bow,* or *The Sign of the Beaver.* Have them decide whether or not Speare's writing style in that book seems similar to that of the passage in this lesson.

➤ Have students create a new scene between Kit and Nathaniel, one in which Nathaniel again thinks he is coming to Kit's rescue.

Three Who's Telling the Story?

Critical Reading

FOCUS

Elizabeth George Speare uses a third-person point of view, concentrating on how Kit Tyler feels:

"A solid cloud of disapproval settled over the dripping girl, more chilling than the April breeze."

BACKGROUND

Point of view is the vantage point from which a story is told. It determines the relationship between the narrator and the story. If the narrator is telling his or her own story, the point of view is typically first person. Explain to students that third-person point of view is more complicated. If the narrator reveals only the thoughts of one or two characters, the point of view is third-person limited. (Mysteries often use this format so that the reader is learning information through the mind of the detective or investigator, but not the criminals.) Other writers choose an omniscient third-person point of view in which the narrator has the ability to see into the minds of all of the characters and record their thoughts. Like a superhuman being, this narrator is all-knowing.

➤ In Lesson Three, students return to the excerpt of *The Witch of Blackbird Pond* to determine which third-person point of view is used, limited or omniscient. They should be able to see that the narrator is limited to the thoughts of Kit Tyler; we are participating in the event through her feelings and thoughts.

FOR DISCUSSION AND REFLECTION

➤ Are there instances in which readers know Kit's feeling or thoughts but the other characters in the story do not? (Yes. Answers may include that she regretted the trip ashore, was grateful to return, was not used to being ignored, felt triumph that she could beat Nathaniel back to the boat, and felt ridiculous by becoming a spectacle.)

➤ How do we know what the other characters feel towards Kit? (Answers may vary. We do not know their thoughts, but we know what they say, their expressions, their look of disapproval or worship, and so on.)

➤ What questions do you have about the selection that remain unanswered? (Possibilities include why Kit is traveling to Connecticut, why Nathaniel is on the ship, and why it is so unusual for Kit to know how to swim.)

Writing

QUICK ASSESS

Do students' narratives:

✓ present a different point of view?

✓ accurately portray the facts?

✓ offer answers to some of their questions?

Collect and display students' unanswered questions before asking them to write about the incident in this excerpt from a different point of view. For example, they might write from the captain's point of view about the nuisance of having to go back and get Kit and Nathaniel. They might write from the little girl's point of view as she watches the loss and then the rescue of her doll.

READING AND WRITING EXTENSIONS

➤ Encourage students to write about a time they got in trouble at school or at home. First, have them write a third-person narrative about the event. Then have them write a first-person account of the same experience.

➤ Invite students to track a current news story for several weeks and collect a variety of articles about it from newspapers or magazines. Have them examine the articles they find to locate third-person and first-person accounts and discuss their impressions of each.

Four **The Plot**

Critical Reading

FOCUS

Some plots have surprising twists at the end.

BACKGROUND

Judith Gorog's "Those Three Wishes" seems a parody of the Aladdin tale, in which a genie grants wishes to a young boy. In Gorog's work, a high school girl is granted three wishes, this time by a magical snail. Most of the story is an internal monologue where Melinda Alice, who has a reputation for her malice, makes self-centered wishes—that her next thousand wishes come true, that she will always be perfectly dressed, that she has pierced ears and small gold earrings, and so on. Early in the story, readers learn that she is going to school early to study for a math test. During her walk to school, she becomes preoccupied with her own wishes and forgets the test. Students will enjoy the irony in her last wish when she remembers that she has a test ahead of her and groans "I wish I were dead."

➤ Students should enjoy identifying the series of events that constitute the plot. In the exposition, readers find out about Melinda Alice's evil nature. The rising action includes all of her wishes. The climax is the classroom scene when, after a classmate reminds her about the test, Melinda makes the fatal wish, and the resolution is left to be inferred.

FOR DISCUSSION AND REFLECTION

➤ What do we learn about Melinda Alice's parents in the exposition? (We find out that her mother hopes her daughter will grow out of her cruelty, and her father thinks that only grades matter. They are not very involved with their daughter.)

➤ What do you think of how the story ends? (Responses will vary, but some students will probably like the abrupt resolution in which we infer that Melinda Alice gets all of her wishes granted, including her wish to die.)

Writing

QUICK ASSESS

Do students' summaries:

✓ cover the entire plot?

✓ use the details from the graphic organizers?

As students explain their graphic organizers of the story, encourage them to make the necessary changes if certain plot events are missing or out of order. Then, using their organizer, students write a summary of the plot.

READING AND WRITING EXTENSIONS

➤ Invite students to read another short story from Judith Gorog's *Please Do Not Touch*, an anthology of creepy tales. Have them look for similarities and differences between the new story and the one in their *Daybooks*.

➤ Invite students to try their hand at an ironic ending with an unexpected twist, by writing their own short story or poem. Remind them that the irony could be verbal, as in "Those Three Wishes," or depend on a surprising event.

See also Answer Key, page 113

Five The Theme

Critical Reading

FOCUS

Readers identify a story's theme after reviewing the plot events, analyzing the characters' reactions, and drawing from their own personal experiences.

BACKGROUND

The focus of this lesson is the significance of theme in fiction. The theme of a story is a lesson about life, a particular truth or underlying meaning. In most stories, the theme arises out of the events of the story—the plot—and out of the interaction of characters in the story.

➤ Some students may not be willing to say that Judith Gorog wants to convey some truth about human life through her character of Melinda Alice and may balk at a discussion of theme. Encourage them to refer back to their original response notes in the previous lesson to find plot events that might lead to a theme statement. Help students realize that readers may interpret the theme differently since theme interpretation is largely based on personal experience.

➤ Other students may be eager to point out possible themes. One might be that an evil person gets punished in the end. Another possible theme that students might suggest is "Watch what you wish for." Melinda Alice has been successful in having all of her wishes come true, and the reader knows her last wish will be granted, too.

FOR DISCUSSION AND REFLECTION

➤ What do we know about Melinda Alice and how she interacts with her peers? (She is called Melinda Malice because she is "clever and cruel." In eighth grade, she had been mean to the "myopic" girl. Her bad behavior continues in high school; there are people she wants to pay back, and she seems to enjoy the power the wishes give her.)

➤ What do you think of the wishes Melinda makes? (Melinda Alice's wishes for a thousand wishes, to be dressed well, and for pierced ears and earrings show her selfishness and a focus on material things. She momentarily thinks of wishing for good things for the world but soon rejects that altruistic feeling.)

Writing

QUICK ASSESS

Do students' journal entries:

✓ focus on a personal experience?

✓ relate the incident to the story's theme?

After listing possible themes on the board, students will write a journal entry. The entry should relate the theme to a personal experience.

READING AND WRITING EXTENSIONS

➤ Encourage students to read the fables of La Fontaine, Aesop, or James Thurber, most of which have explicit themes or morals stated at the end. Have them write a modern day fable for eighth graders.

➤ Ask students to change the ending of "Those Three Wishes" so that Melinda does not wish to be dead but instead continues on her wishing spree at school. Have students share these endings with classmates and compare them to the original. How was the theme altered by the new conclusions?

See also Answer Key, page 113

Unit Overview

This unit presents students with strategies for unlocking the theme in poetry, fables, and short stories. As they ask questions about and examine textual details from selections by Gwendolyn Brooks, James Thurber, and Ernest Hemingway, students will gain skills in identifying primary and secondary themes and in explaining their significance.

Literature Focus

	Lesson	Literature
1.	Finding the Theme	**Gwendolyn Brooks,** from *Blacks* (Fiction)
2.	Themes in Poems	**Gwendolyn Brooks,** "Pete at the Zoo" (Poetry)
3.	Themes in Fables	**James Thurber,** "The Princess and the Tin Box" (Fable)
4.	The Main Message	**Ernest Hemingway,** "A Day's Wait" (Short Story)
5.	The Secondary Message	

Reading Focus

1. As you read a piece of writing, think to yourself, "What is the writer saying to me?" When you answer that question, you will know the theme.

2. As you read a poem, look for images that contribute to the theme. Deciding why the writer chose those particular images will help you discover the theme.

3. The theme of a piece of writing is the author's underlying message about life. In fables, the moral can help you understand the theme.

4. The primary theme is the most prominent or important theme in a story. To find it, make a mental list of all the themes and choose the one that makes the most sense with the details in the story.

5. As you read, look for additional themes beyond the primary one. These secondary themes can add to your understanding of the story.

Writing Focus

1. Explain how details from a story support the theme.
2. Reflect on the imagery of a poem.
3. Rewrite the end of a fable.
4. Summarize the primary theme of a story.
5. Plan a story about a childhood experience.

One Finding the Theme

Critical Reading

FOCUS

D.H. Melhem, a literary critic, believes that Gwendolyn Brooks, "enriches both black and white cultures by revealing essential life, its universal identities, and the challenge it poses to a society beset with corruption and decay."

BACKGROUND

Gwendolyn Brooks (1917–), a major contemporary poet, was the first African American writer to win a Pulitzer Prize. She is "best known for her sensitive portraits of urban blacks who encounter racism and poverty in their daily lives."

➤ Lesson One presents a description of a ghetto neighborhood from *Blacks*, a fictional work. In it, Brooks first describes the happy, young children of Thirty-fourth Street as "blooms," and then she describes the tragic, middle-aged men who have reached a dead-end life there. Help students look for Brooks's theme by analyzing details that she emphasizes or by looking at the organization of the piece. For example, discuss with students why she set off an entire sentence for emphasis in the third paragraph: "Those men were going no further—and had gone nowhere. Tragedy." Possible theme statements for the piece include that a worthwhile life has a worthy tragedy or that one should look for the humor, even in the bad times.

FOR DISCUSSION AND REFLECTION

➤ Does Maud Martha seem to be an optimist or a pessimist? (Answers will vary. Students who feel she is optimistic may point to her belief that "life was more comedy than tragedy" and that almost everything has a comic dimension. Those who feel she is pessimistic may mention her opinion that "if you got a good Tragedy out of a lifetime, one good, ripping tragedy . . . you were doing very well.")

➤ Why would tragedy be good in life? (Answers will vary but may include ideas that at least you have experienced life to a full degree.)

➤ Have students discuss their views of tragedy. Have they or anyone they know experienced a personal tragedy?

Writing

QUICK ASSESS

Do students' responses:

✓ explain how details support the theme?

✓ reflect a thoughtful reading of the story?

After stating the theme in their own words, students will explain how certain details support Brooks's theme. Remind students that different readers may perceive the theme of a work differently.

READING AND WRITING EXTENSIONS

➤ Encourage students to read more poetry of Gwendolyn Brooks—perhaps poems from *A Street in Bronzeville* or *Annie Allen*. Ask them to consider the themes of these poems.

➤ Invite students to react to Maud Martha's belief that one can usually "find something to laugh at in almost every situation." Do they agree with her? Why or why not?

See also Answer Key, page 113

Two Themes in Poems

Critical Reading

FOCUS

A poem's symbols and images often contain clues to its theme.

BACKGROUND

In Lesson Two, students explore the themes in poems by focusing on the poet's use of images and symbols. "Pete at the Zoo," by Gwendolyn Brooks, deals with the topic of appearance vs. reality by expressing the idea that what people see outwardly does not always reflect what is inside. On the surface, the poem seems to describe an elephant at the zoo who, during the day, is visited by shouting boys and girls and stamps his foot in a show of "might." However, Brooks's description makes the reader wonder about the elephant in the absence of the recognition and company provided by the zoo visitors. In the last line, the reader discovers the speaker is really describing herself, when she hunches up "Against the dark of night."

FOR DISCUSSION AND REFLECTION

➤ What images does Brooks use to develop the mood of the poem? (The mood is pensive and questioning, developed through words like "lonely,"and "no one" and the final question, "Does he hunch up as I do / Against the dark of night?")

➤ What do you think of the speaker of the poem? (Answers may focus on her insecurities, her empathy for the elephant. Students may have been surprised to discover that what seemed to be a description of an elephant was a self-description.)

➤ How is the elephant different at night? (Answers should include that the elephant is lonely and afraid, not the center of attention as he is during the day.)

➤ Ask students to consider why Brooks might have chosen to write about an elephant, as opposed to any other animal.

Writing

QUICK ASSESS

Do students' explanations:

✓ comment on the speaker's feelings about herself?

✓ comment on the theme of appearance vs. reality?

After students share their ideas about how the image of the elephant connects to what Brooks is trying to say about life, suggest that they work in groups to reflect on the speaker's feelings about herself and the contrast between appearance and reality.

READING AND WRITING EXTENSIONS

➤ Ask students to write a poem, using "Pete at the Zoo" as a model, about another zoo animal. Suggest that they think about what the animal might be like at night, when the crowds have gone.

➤ Invite students to browse through their *Daybooks* and select one of the photographs that intrigues them. Have them describe the images they see and offer a title to accompany the picture.

See also Answer Key, page 113

Three Themes in Fables

Critical Reading

FOCUS

From *Junior Discovering Authors*:

"Although he took great pride in his literary accomplishments, Thurber made no attempt to write a 'serious' work; he was content with his reputation as an author of diverting light sketches."

BACKGROUND

James Thurber (1894–1961) was one of the foremost humorists in American literature. His modern fables, like "The Unicorn in the Garden" and "The Night the Bed Fell," display his talent for social satire with an eccentric comic element. Thurber's work offers a good example of this lesson's subject, the author's direct statement of theme. Thurber often imitated Aesop's fables, directly stating a moral at the end of the story. However, Thurber's morals are often unexpected, as he offers a twist at the end.

➤ As they examine the surprise moral in "The Princess and the Tin Box," students may have to work harder than they expect to unravel the theme. The expected outcome would be that the beautiful princess would select the ordinary tin box containing commonplace rocks. That would indicate that she is not a materialistic young woman. Ironically, she chooses the bejeweled box, and Thurber rattles the reader with his statement about staying after class and writing on the blackboard. Students may be surprised by Thurber's suggestion that modern man is materialistic.

FOR DISCUSSION AND REFLECTION

➤ Where do you first see that Thurber has used language not found in the traditional fable? (Responses will vary. Some students may note the mention of "Cartier's window" or the concern that the princess not use "cheap" materials.)

➤ What motivated the princess to select the sapphire jewel box from the other expensive gifts? (She says, "It is a very large and expensive box, and when I am married, I will meet many admirers who will give me precious gems with which to fill it to the top." In other words, she is motivated by materialism and greed.)

Writing

QUICK ASSESS

Do students' fables:

✓ have a new ending?

✓ present a new moral or theme?

After discussing Thurber's theme, students rewrite the fable with a different ending—that is, the princess chooses a different suitor. After they state the new moral or lesson, have them discuss the variations with classmates.

READING AND WRITING EXTENSIONS

➤ Encourage students to read another of Thurber's fables from *Fables for Our Time* or *Further Fables for Our Time*. Have them report to the class on the themes.

➤ Invite students to write social commentary of their lives as eighth graders in fable form. Have them set the fables in a familiar setting—the school, a nearby park, a popular restaurant, a particular store. Encourage students to surprise the readers with their morals.

See also Answer Key, page 114

Four The Main Message

Critical Reading

FOCUS

The events and the characters' reactions can point to the theme or underlying meaning of a work of fiction.

BACKGROUND

Lesson Four is designed to help students determine the primary theme of a story. Readers' responses and thoughts about text usually lead to several possible meanings for literature, but one of these themes usually emerges above the others.

➤ The story "A Day's Wait" is by Ernest Hemingway (1899–1961), lauded as one of the greatest American writers of the twentieth century. This short story relates a day in the life of a young boy who is sick with fever, possibly influenza. He overhears the doctor state that he has a fever of 102 degrees. Without telling his fear to his father, he believes he is going to die because of his high temperature. At the story's end, readers learn that he has confused the Celsius and Fahrenheit measurement scales. Once the boy communicates with his father, he realizes his error.

➤ To narrow the theme to the primary one, students should decide what Schatz and/or his father learned from the experience. Possibilities would be not to jump to conclusions, to reveal your fears honestly, to communicate more openly, to be careful you do not misunderstand something, and so on. After choosing a primary theme, encourage students to support it with evidence from the story.

FOR DISCUSSION AND REFLECTION

➤ Why does Schatz say, "You don't have to stay in here with me, Papa, if it bothers you"? (The boy feels he is dying and is trying to spare his father the horror of witnessing death.)

➤ What information has confused Schatz? (Because Schatz had confused the two systems for measuring temperature, he assumed that his high fever meant certain death.)

➤ Why would Schatz cry very easily the next day? (He need not be strong any longer. He relaxes what Hemingway calls his "hold over himself.")

Writing

QUICK ASSESS

Do students' summaries:

✓ identify a primary theme of the short story?

✓ explain why the theme is important?

Using response notes and class discussion notes, students should work in small groups to generate many possible themes of the story before summarizing the one that they believe to be the primary meaning.

READING AND WRITING EXTENSIONS

➤ Invite students to research the life and death of Ernest Hemingway. Have them share information with the class that they find interesting.

➤ Have students write about a time when they or someone in their family was very ill. Can they make personal connections between Hemingway's characters and themselves and their family? Do they ever recall feeling as scared as Schatz does?

See also Answer Key, page 114

Five The Secondary Message

Critical Reading

FOCUS

Identifying secondary themes can enhance your enjoyment of a literary work.

BACKGROUND

Lesson Five is intended to help students explore the secondary themes in the literature they read. Suggest that students revisit the list of themes they made in the previous lesson.

➤ Emphasize to students that they will need to find supporting textual evidence for any secondary theme they propose.

➤ Ernest Hemingway has often been considered the "master of understated prose style," and "A Day's Wait" certainly exemplifies this technique. Understatement is saying less. What is not said between the father and the son is as important as what they do say.

FOR DISCUSSION AND REFLECTION

➤ What questions should the boy have asked his father? (Answers may include exactly how sick he is, what a high temperature means, and if he is going to die.)

➤ How do you know that the father did not understand the extent of the boy's fear? (Responses may include that he did not understand why Schatz was not following the oral reading of the story. He left the room at the boy's request. If the father had really known the boy feared his own death, the father certainly would have stayed.)

➤ Which of the possible secondary themes listed on page 67 is the most reasonable? (Answers will vary.)

Writing

QUICK ASSESS

Do students' plans:

✔ describe a particular event?

✔ express primary and secondary themes?

✔ list people who were involved?

Students are asked to plan their own memoir of a childhood event that taught them something important. Before they begin to list people involved and possible themes, have the class brainstorm different possible events in their lives—happy as well as sad experiences.

READING AND WRITING EXTENSIONS

➤ Suggest that students use their plans to actually write their stories. Ask them to invite classmates to read the finished works. Have them discuss whether the primary theme the author intended to convey was successfully communicated to readers.

➤ Encourage students to go back to Thurber's "The Princess and the Tin Box" (pages 60–61). Have each student list possible secondary themes of the fable and then compare their lists with those of their classmates.

See also Answer Key, page 114

Unit Overview

This unit looks at the use of compressed and concentrated language in poetry and fiction. As they read and respond to works by Eve Merriam, Seamus Heaney, Robert Frost, and William Saroyan, students will examine the various ways that writers create comparisons through similes and metaphors, establish sound patterns, present a mood, and use symbols.

Literature Focus

	Lesson	Literature
1.	Simile	**Eve Merriam,** "Simile: Willow and Ginkgo" (Poetry)
2.	Metaphor	**Seamus Heaney,** "Scaffolding" (Poetry)
3.	Assonance, Consonance, and Alliteration	**Robert Frost,** "Fire and Ice" (Poetry)
4.	Setting the Mood	**William Saroyan,** "Gaston" (Short Story)
5.	Symbolism	**William Saroyan,** "Gaston" (Short Story)

Reading Focus

1. Writers use similes to bring a freshness and a sense of surprise to their writing.
2. Metaphors can bring freshness and vitality to a poem. An extended metaphor can help unify the entire poem.
3. When you read a poem, notice how assonance, consonance, and alliteration are used to enhance meaning.
4. Setting and word choice often enhance a story's mood.
5. Recognizing symbols can help make abstractions more concrete and easier to understand.

Writing Focus

1. Following a model, write a poem using similes.
2. Explain a poem's final stanza.
3. Write a one-stanza poem using a combination of assonance, consonance, and alliteration.
4. Explain the techniques an author uses to create mood in a story.
5. Explain the meaning of a symbol in a story.

One Simile

Critical Reading

FOCUS

Similes can help readers see familiar things in a new way:

"The willow's music is like a soprano / Delicate and thin."

BACKGROUND

The title of Laurence Perrine's textbook, *Sound and Sense,* is really the core of this lesson about looking at how writers choose the words they use. Some students may be skeptical about the amount of planning writers do but try to persuade them that the best writers often make conscious decisions about what particular words to choose and how to arrange them.

➤ Remind students that a simile is a comparison using *like* or *as.* Eve Merriam uses an abundance of similes in her poem, "Simile: Willow and Gingko," and students should have little difficulty picking them out. The entire poem is organized to contrast the two trees. To emphasize their differences, Merriam selects strongly different similes. The willow is "like an etching," "like a soprano," and "sleek as a velvet-nosed calf," while the ginkgo is "like a crude sketch," "like a chorus," and "like stubby rough wool." Students need to recognize the appeal of each.

FOR DISCUSSION AND REFLECTION

➤ What does Merriam mean that her "eyes feast upon the willow," but her "heart goes to the ginkgo"? (Answers will vary. The willow is described in artistic terms— such as an etching or a soprano, protected and precious. In contrast, the ginkgo is described as less visually appealing, but as strong and determined: "Like a city child, it grows up in the street. / Thrust against the metal sky, / Somehow it survives and even thrives.")

➤ What sensory imagery do you find striking? (Responses will vary. Help students see that Merriam appeals to sight ("like an etching / Fine-lined against the sky" or "like a crude sketch"), to touch ("like silken thread" or "like stubby rough wool"), and also to sound ("like a soprano / Delicate and thin" or "like a chorus / With everyone joining in.")

Writing

QUICK ASSESS

Do students' poems:

✓ follow the model?

✓ use vivid similes to contrast the two topics?

After discussing the similes of the poem and how they establish detailed differences between the two trees, students create their own similes, make sketches or pictures to show the connections between the two different objects being compared, and create a poem modeled after "Simile: Willow and Gingko."

READING AND WRITING EXTENSIONS

➤ Encourage students to use Merriam's descriptions to draw a sketch of the two trees. Then show students illustrations from a tree identification book for comparison.

➤ Invite students to be "simile detectives" for a week. Ask them to find similes in stories, books, newspapers, or magazines and to listen for similes in conversation, song lyrics, and commercials. Have students bring their lists of similes to post on a bulletin board for all to see.

Two Metaphor

Critical Reading

FOCUS

Robert Frost on the power of poetry:

"Poetry provides the one permissible way of saying one thing and meaning another."

BACKGROUND

Like simile, metaphor also is a figure of speech used by poets to make comparisons, a way of going beyond the literal and adding dimension to description. "Scaffolding," by Seamus Heaney, compares two unlike things—a permanent relationship between two people and the scaffolding used in building construction. Because the comparison is maintained throughout the poem, it is called an extended metaphor or a sustained metaphor.

➤ Help students to see that people use metaphors frequently in their everyday speech. Poets can add freshness to their imagery by creating unusual, provocative comparisons, as Heaney has done in "Scaffolding." If possible, show students a picture of the scaffolding used in construction sites or renovations to help them envision what Heaney is writing about.

FOR DISCUSSION AND REFLECTION

➤ Is scaffolding a good image with which to describe building a relationship? (Answers may vary. While scaffolding is temporary, it is often necessary in order to work on the solid building behind it: "And yet all this comes down when the job's done / Showing off walls of sure and solid stone.")

➤ What could scaffolds refer to in real life? (Possible answers include problems between people, arguments, disagreements, moving away from each other, passage of time, and so on.)

➤ What might the "old bridges breaking" refer to? (Students will have various ideas, but possible answers may be rifts in opinion, disagreements, or physical distance between the speaker and the "dear" he is addressing.)

Writing

QUICK ASSESS

Do students' explanations:

✔ reflect on the metaphor of the poem?

✔ interpret the final two lines?

Have students work in groups to visualize the extended metaphor of the poem before they explain the last two lines. Suggest that they look for details from the poem (planks, ladders, walls, bridges, and so on) in the sketches they have made.

READING AND WRITING EXTENSIONS

➤ Encourage students to read and respond to other poems that have extended or sustained metaphors, such as Robert Frost's "A Hillside Thaw" or Langston Hughes's "Mother to Son."

➤ Invite students to create an original metaphor to describe their relationship with a good friend or close family member. Encourage them to illustrate their metaphors and share them with classmates.

See also Answer Key, page 114

Three Assonance, Consonance, and Alliteration

Critical Reading

FOCUS

Edgar Allan Poe describes poetry as "music ... combined with a pleasurable idea."

BACKGROUND

Among the language devices poetry draws upon to develop its meaning are the use of sound patterns—the musical techniques of *assonance*, the repetition of vowel sounds within words; *consonance*, the repetition of consonant sounds anywhere within words; and *alliteration*, the repetition of initial consonant sounds. Why all of this attention to the letters within words? The sounds that poets choose to use enhance or reinforce the meaning of the poetry.

➤ You may need to explain that hard sounds like *k*, hard *c*, or hard *g*, *d*, and *t* create one mood for poetry, while soft sounds like *w*, *wh*, *s*, and *fl* create another. When a writer wants a soft mood for a love song, soft sounds are used. When a writer wants a harsh sound to make a point, the hard sounds are used. It may work well to use a popular song to demonstrate further the use of sound devices.

➤ In Frost's "Fire and Ice," an example of alliteration is the *s* and *w* in the line "Some say the world will end in fire." An example of assonance is in the strong long-*I* sound in *fire*, *ice*, *desire*, *twice*, and *suffice*. An example of repeated consonant sounds is in the *s* throughout the poem.

FOR DISCUSSION AND REFLECTION

➤ How do the sounds of the poem contribute to its meaning? (The poet uses alliteration, consonance, and assonance to make the poem sound almost like a nursery rhyme. Frost seems to want to use a simple vehicle to get across a universal truth or idea, that the world will end by fire or ice.)

➤ What are some examples of sound devices used in the poem? (Students need to cite specific words and phrases.)

➤ How would you describe the mood of the poem? (Responses will vary.)

Writing

QUICK ASSESS

Do students' poems:

✓ use one or more of the sound devices?

✓ match the sound to meaning?

After students generate lists of words containing assonance and consonance, they will select a topic and develop a one-stanza poem using the sound devices. Remind them of the importance of matching the sound to the meaning.

READING AND WRITING EXTENSIONS

➤ Invite students to bring in the printed lyrics of songs from cassettes and CDs. In small groups, have them share, analyze, and present examples of assonance, consonance, and alliteration that they have found.

➤ Encourage students to share their poetry orally so that classmates can "hear" the devices. Invite peers to give written feedback.

Four Setting the Mood

Critical Reading

FOCUS
A writer employs a variety of techniques to create mood, including description of the setting, word choice, and character reaction.

BACKGROUND

In Lesson Four, students explore how the mood of a piece of fiction may be established through description of the setting, word choice, and characters' reactions. The mood of the first part of "Gaston" is lighthearted, casual, and friendly.

➤ William Saroyan (1901–1982), an American writer, is probably best known for his Pulitzer Prize-winning play *The Time of Your Life* (1939). However, he also wrote many short stories. Howard Floan described Saroyan's fictional style by noting his "indifference to plot, his preference for outcasts, his contempt for formal education, and his distrust of creeds combined with a nearly mystical reverence for life." Many of these elements are seen in this lesson's excerpt of "Gaston." The character of Papa certainly is the estranged father and outcast, living on his own in Paris. He reveres all life, even the seed dweller within the peach and tries to communicate this with his six-year-old daughter.

FOR DISCUSSION AND REFLECTION

➤ What is the mood of this piece? (It is lighthearted, friendly, relaxed, and casual. Students might point to the description of the father as "kind of funny," the details that they are both barefoot, and that the father names and makes up a story for Gaston as evidence of the pleasant mood.)

➤ How do the father's actions surprise his daughter? (He does not kill the seed dweller, and he eats the rest of the peach even after he has found the bug. This is contrary to life as she knows it.)

➤ Where does the story take place? (Answers may include in an apartment in Paris, on a hot August day, close to small neighborhood shops.)

Writing

QUICK ASSESS

Do students' responses:

✓ list techniques used by Saroyan?

✓ explain how the techniques develop the mood?

✓ comment on the setting?

To help students explain the techniques Saroyan uses to create mood, encourage students to gather details from the story. Have one group work on details about setting, another on character description, another on word choice in dialogue, and another on character reaction. Each group should come up with words to describe the setting based on the details collected.

READING AND WRITING EXTENSIONS

➤ Encourage students to read more of the writings of William Saroyan—his short stories, his plays, or his novels—and share their impressions with the class.

➤ Invite students to reread "Those Three Wishes" by Judith Gorog (page 49). How did Gorog develop the mood through the different reactions of the characters?

Five Symbolism

Critical Reading

FOCUS
Laurence Perrine on symbols:

"Meanings ray out from a symbol like the corona around the sun, or like connotations around a richly suggestive word. But the very fact that a symbol may be so rich in its meaning makes it necessary that we use the greatest tact in its interpretation."

BACKGROUND
In Lesson Five, students read the second part of Saroyan's "Gaston" as they consider how writers use symbolism. Perhaps because symbols often seem less precise than other figures of speech (such as simile and metaphor) and more open to interpretation, students may find understanding the function of symbols especially difficult. Remind students that symbols can have more than one interpretation. For example, the flag could represent our country, democracy, the fifty states, the thirteen colonies, patriotism, and so on.

FOR DISCUSSION AND REFLECTION
➤ Ask students if they noticed that the mother's opinion of the father is somewhat like the little girl's opinion of Gaston. (The mother says that the father "makes up a lot of foolishness," and the little girl's first impression of Gaston, is that "he was silly and wrong and ridiculous and useless and all sorts of other things.")

➤ How has the girl treated Gaston and her father similarly? (She has rejected them both. She squishes the bug, and she leaves the father even though she has said she wanted to stay with him.)

➤ Why did the father say that he was "feeling a little . . . like Gaston on the white plate"? (Students may respond that Gaston had been displaced from his home in the peach, while the father is also an outcast, displaced in Paris away from his child.)

➤ What does the mother think about the father? (She feels he is odd and often expresses strange ideas.)

Writing

QUICK ASSESS
Do students' responses:

✓ clearly agree or disagree with the statement?

✓ provide supporting details from the story?

✓ comment on the story's symbolism?

After students complete a web comparing the father and Gaston, have students write an essay that agrees or disagrees with this statement: "Gaston symbolizes the father's loneliness."

READING AND WRITING EXTENSIONS
➤ Have students imagine they are writing a poem about an abstraction, such as loneliness, happiness, success, or jealousy. Ask them to select a symbol that they might use to help readers understand their theme more easily. Encourage students to share and explain their choices with classmates.

➤ Invite students to rewrite the ending of "Gaston." What would happen if the girl refused to return to New York with her mother and remained in Paris with her father?

See also Answer Key, page 115

Unit Overview

In this unit, students explore the strategies of examining an argument. As they read a variety of nonfiction, students will learn how writers look at both sides of an issue, choose one viewpoint, appeal to the readers' emotions, and support their positions persuasively with examples, reasons, and observations. Students will learn to respond to opposing viewpoints and develop their abilities to distinguish between fact and opinion as they plan arguments of their own.

Literature Focus

	Lesson	Literature
1.	Taking a Position	"Memorial and Recommendations of the Grand Council Fire of American Indians" (Nonfiction)
2.	Reasons and Evidence	
3.	The Other Side	**Dan Rather,** "Silencing the Sound of Music" (Nonfiction)
4.	Facts and Opinions	**Andy Rooney,** "America the Not-so-Beautiful" (Nonfiction)
5.	Weighing an Argument	

Reading Focus

1. Identifying the thesis statement in a written argument helps readers to understand the author's thinking.
2. Readers can analyze written arguments by identifying the reasons and evidence.
3. An effective argument deals with both sides of an issue.
4. Recognizing facts and opinions helps readers evaluate written arguments.
5. Readers can evaluate an argument by examining its appeals to reason and to emotion.

Writing Focus

1. Explain your view of a thesis statement.
2. Respond to an argument.
3. Create a bumper sticker expressing your view on an issue.
4. Explain and evaluate how a writer supports his opinions.
5. Write an argument that appeals to feelings and to reason and anticipates opposing opinions.

One Taking a Position

Critical Reading

FOCUS

The thesis statement of an argument expresses the main idea:

"The Indian has long been hurt by these unfair books. We ask only that our story be told in fairness."

BACKGROUND

In Lesson One, students examine a letter written by American Indians in 1927 about the portrait of Indians that was presented in textbooks for schoolchildren. The authors of the letter at the Grand Council Fire argue for the truth to be told about the American Indian. Students need to read the letter and find the thesis—that the history of Indians presented in textbooks is unfair—repeated at the beginning and the ending.

➤ It may be useful to present enough historical background so that students understand that the rights of Native Americans were only beginning to increase in the 1920s. Universal Indian citizenship had only become law in 1924. Prior to this, citizenship was awarded on an individual basis, although it was taken for granted by all whites in America. In the 1920s, there was a backlash by American Indians to the missionary schools on the reservations. Many Native Americans felt those schools—and their textbooks—had promoted Indian assimilation at the cost of the dissolution of the Indian tribal cultures.

FOR DISCUSSION AND REFLECTION

➤ What language used in the textbooks do the Indians feel is unfair? (Answers may include that the Indian victories are called "massacres," that Indians acting in self-defense are called "murderers," that Indians are called "thieves" while they live with few possessions, and they are called "savages," although they are a "civilized race.")

➤ What details do the American Indians suggest should be added to textbooks? (Possible answers include their knowledge of handicrafts, their songs, their games, their orators, their leaders and heroes.)

Writing

QUICK ASSESS

Do students' responses:

✓ express their opinion of the thesis?

✓ use evidence from the text?

After students identify the thesis statement (that there is a need to write more fairly about the Indians in textbooks), they will explain whether they agree or disagree with the thesis. Encourage students to use details from the letter to support their ideas.

READING AND WRITING EXTENSIONS

➤ Encourage students to read at least part of a novel about Native Americans— perhaps *The Education of Little Tree*, by Forrest Carter; *A Yellow Raft on Blue Water* by Michael Dorris; *I Heard the Owl Call My Name* by Margaret Craven; or *The Light in the Forest*, by Conrad Richter. Have them share their impressions with the class.

➤ The authors of the letter state that they want their story to "be told in fairness." Invite students to think about other groups whose history and culture may not be presented fairly in history textbooks or encyclopedias. Encourage them to share their views with classmates.

See also Answer Key, page 115

Two Reasons and Evidence

Critical Reading

FOCUS

Before agreeing with the argument of a persuasive essay, consider the evidence given to support the reasons.

BACKGROUND

The second lesson again focuses on the letter from the Grand Council Fire of American Indians. Here students are asked to focus on the evidence that the Indians offer as support for their view that textbooks are unfair. Remind students that evidence can be facts, statistics, examples, observations, quotations, and opinions—although not all of these are used in the letter. An example of an observation would be "no mention is made of broken treaties on the part of the white man." Other evidence is based on examples, such as that "Indians killed white men because white men took their lands, ruined their hunting grounds, burned their forests, destroyed their buffalo."

FOR DISCUSSION AND REFLECTION

➤ What evidence supports that the Indians are civilized people, not savages? (Answers might include handicrafts, songs, great statesmen and orators, games, legends, and proverbs.)

➤ What additional evidence might have made the argument more persuasive? (Students will have various opinions. Encourage them to be specific about the particular facts, examples, statistics, or observations they think would strengthen the argument.)

➤ What evidence do you find most persuasive? (Students should explain the reasons behind their choices.)

Writing

QUICK ASSESS

Do students' explanations:

✓ comment on the changes recommended in the letter?

✓ support their reasons with evidence?

Students should work in small groups to complete the chart about the reasons and evidence. Have each group present their reasons and evidence to the class before students write about whether they believe the changes recommended in the letter have occurred.

READING AND WRITING EXTENSIONS

➤ Encourage students to investigate some of the historical references made in the letter—the battle with General Custer, the Battle at Wounded Knee, or Indian leaders and heroes such as Black Partridge and Shabbona.

➤ Suggest that students create a dialogue between one of the Indian leaders at the Grand Council Fire and Jesse B. Simple, from Langston Hughes's newspaper column (page 17). Have them consider how Simple might react to the complaints in the letter.

See also Answer Key, page 115

Three The Other Side

Critical Reading

FOCUS

Effective writers recognize that every issue has two sides:

"These observations are shared with a hope: that, when schools cut back on music classes, they really think about what they're doing—and don't take music for granted."

BACKGROUND
Students may recognize Dan Rather as the CBS News anchorman for *The CBS Evening News with Dan Rather* and the host of *48 Hours*. You may want to fill in more of his background as a veteran news reporter for CBS who has covered all of the major historical events of the last thirty years, including the assassination of President Kennedy, the Vietnam War, Watergate, and all of the presidential elections since 1964.

➤ "The Other Side" presents Rather in a different light, as an author of an argument supporting music education in schools. His thesis appears in the third paragraph: "I have begun to wonder if our easy access to music has made it too easy for us to take music for granted." Rather offers his own personal experience in elementary school to support his belief in music education. Help students to see that Rather effectively anticipates what the critics will say: "Music seems like a frivolity when you compare it to chemistry labs . . . ."

FOR DISCUSSION AND REFLECTION
➤ What is Rather's attitude toward his own musical ability? (He shows humility and humor: "Scholars believe the wood block was invented *before* music. And if you needed proof of that, you had only to listen to the way I played.")

➤ What opposing arguments does Rather anticipate? (Answers should include that music is not as important as subjects like chemistry, that instruments are expensive, and that music is merely an elective.)

➤ How persuasive do you find Rather's argument? What sort of things have you learned in school music classes? (Responses will vary.)

Writing

QUICK ASSESS

Do students' creations:

✓ express a view about music education?

✓ show care and planning?

After discussing the details Rather uses to argue for music education, students create a bumper sticker that would express their views on the subject of music education.

READING AND WRITING EXTENSIONS
➤ Invite students to investigate the music expenditures of their own school district. Have them make a graphic to show how much money is allocated to music education (instruments, supplies, teachers, and so on) compared to areas such as sports or art.

➤ Tape one of the commentaries by Dan Rather on the *CBS Evening News*. Bring it to class and ask students to analyze its thesis, Rather's use of evidence, and his anticipation of opposing viewpoints.

Four Facts and Opinions

Critical Reading

FOCUS

While writers may use opinions and observations to enliven writing, a critical reader should look for facts to support an opinion before agreeing with it.

BACKGROUND

In this lesson, students will explore the strategies of separating fact from opinion in an argument. Remind them that facts can be documented in a source beyond the reading and that the critical reader should discern where opinion stops and facts take over.

➤ Students may or may not be familiar with Andy Rooney as a commentator on *60 Minutes*. His style of speaking and writing are easily recognizable—a "crisp, wry combination of humor, carefully selected anecdote, and common-sense wisdom." While this essay looks at the serious problem of polluting the earth with garbage, Rooney's final solution reflects his wit and sometimes sarcastic mocking of American culture.

FOR DISCUSSION AND REFLECTION

➤ What is the thesis of Rooney's essay? (He states that throwing away is the American way, but the problem is that there is "no 'away' left.")

➤ What facts in the essay could be checked? (In addition to the facts listed on page 98, students may list facts such as that Rooney stores chemicals in his garage or that the money Americans spend on food packaging exceeds the income that American farmers make by growing the food.)

➤ What do you think of what Rooney calls "the best solution" in his last paragraph? (Responses will vary.)

Writing

QUICK ASSESS

Do students' paragraphs?

✓ identify the support Rooney gives?

✓ explain whether they have been convinced by the argument?

Have students outline the paragraph in which Rooney calls some manufacturers "evil" for deliberately polluting groundwater. Examining facts and opinions in that paragraph will help prepare them to write a short paragraph evaluating Rooney's argument.

READING AND WRITING EXTENSIONS

➤ Encourage students to watch an Andy Rooney segment on *60 Minutes*. Have them record the topic, paraphrase his line of argument, and explain to the class how well it was supported by facts or opinions. (Earlier editorials can be found on the Internet.)

➤ Invite students to read from Andy Rooney's *A Bird's Eye View of America* travelogue and write a paragraph about their impressions of his style and humor.

See also Answer Key, page 116

Five Weighing an Argument

Critical Reading

FOCUS

A strong argumentative or persuasive essay includes evidence that appeals to both emotions and logic.

BACKGROUND

"Weighing an Argument" is designed to help students evaluate an argument by examining its appeal to both reason and feelings. A writer may try to persuade a reader by using emotionally charged words or appeal to feelings through humor or basic values. Students should be wary of this line of argument, for it may not have real facts to substantiate it. On the other hand, a writer may present a logical argument, using evidence that can be investigated and proven. While this kind of argument may not have a tone as appealing as the first, the reader can more objectively evaluate its truth. The best argument will combine an appealing tone with reliable evidence.

FOR DISCUSSION AND REFLECTION

➤ How do the authors in this unit use emotional appeal to sway the audience? (Answers may include that the Grand Council tries to appeal to basic values, that Dan Rather draws on personal memories, and that Andy Rooney uses humor for appeal.)

➤ How effectively do the authors use facts or evidence to support their arguments? (Answers will vary. Students may note that the Grand Council states the battle of Custer has been taught as a massacre, that Rather states that school districts cut music out of their budgets first, and that Andy Rooney gives the yearly weight of garbage thrown out by each New York City resident.)

➤ Which of the three arguments do you find least convincing? Why? (Encourage students to cite specifics as they explain their views.)

Writing

QUICK ASSESS

Do students' arguments:

✔ present a clear thesis?

✔ use appeals to emotion and to logic?

✔ anticipate opposing viewpoints?

After analyzing appeals to reason and feelings in the readings of this unit, students will write their own argument on one of the three topics: the presentation of Native Americans in American textbooks, the importance of music in a school's curriculum, or the need to stop the dumping of refuse.

READING AND WRITING EXTENSIONS

➤ Encourage students to analyze the emotional appeals of two or three television commercials or magazine advertisements.

➤ Invite students, in groups, to watch and videotape one of the many shows offering two viewpoints on a topic—trials such as *People's Court* and *Judge Judy* or political discussion shows such as *Crossfire, Evans and Novak,* and *Equal Time.* Have them outline the key arguments and explain what they did or didn't find persuasive.

See also Answer Key, page 116

Unit Overview

This unit centers on the work of Cynthia Rylant and the concept of perspective, the way the writer looks at the world. By examining excerpts of a novel, one of her poems, and selections from her autobiography, students piece together the experiences and influences that shaped Rylant's perspective as a sensitive outsider.

Literature Focus

	Lesson	Literature
1.	Characters in Perspective	from *Missing May* (Fiction)
2.	Perspective and Style	from *Missing May* (Fiction)
3.	Perspective and Theme	"Sandy Jane Meador" (Poetry)
4.	Perspective in Autobiography	from *But I'll Be Back Again* (Autobiography)
5.	Reflecting on Perspective	from *But I'll Be Back Again* (Autobiography)

Reading Focus

1. Looking carefully at what story characters say and think can help you understand an author's perspective.
2. Looking at style—an author's unique way of using language—can help you understand more about perspective.
3. Exploring the themes of stories and poems can help you gain insights into an author's perspective.
4. Knowing about an author's background can help you better understand the author's perspective.
5. When you read autobiographies, look for reflections that might explain the author's perspective.

Writing Focus

1. Examine an author's perspective.
2. Write about how Rylant's style affects your understanding of a character's perspective.
3. Explore the theme of a poem.
4. Write about your understanding of Rylant's perspective.
5. Write a journal entry about a previous experience that shaped your perspective.

One Characters in Perspective

Critical Reading

FOCUS

Cynthia Rylant on her characters:

"It is called sensitivity, this quality that sets them apart ....If they possess only a little-more-than-reasonable-amount, they can see into things more deeply than other people."

BACKGROUND

Cynthia Rylant is an award-winning author whose work for children and young adults includes picture books, poetry, short stories, and novels. With a style that has been described as "unadorned, clear, and lyrical," Rylant presents characters with sensitivity. Born in 1952, in rustic West Virginia, Rylant spent much of her childhood with her single mother in the poverty of Appalachia. Help students to see that Rylant's life provided much material for *Missing May*, which won the 1993 Newbery Award.

➤ "Characters in Perspective" shows students what they can find out about an author through his or her choice of characters. The details with which Rylant describes a character reveal much about the sensitivity and the romanticism of the writer herself. For example, Summer, the twelve-year-old narrator, notices the artist in Ob as she first views the whirligigs he has creatively placed throughout the trailer. Summer romanticizes the poverty of the area by describing the rusty old trailer as "a toy that God had been playing with and accidentally dropped out of heaven."

FOR DISCUSSION AND REFLECTION

➤ Would Ob and May make a good family for Summer? Why or why not? (Students will probably believe they would. Encourage them to point to particular details, such as when May plans where to put the swing or Ob plans a tree house.)

➤ How does Summer respond to the whirligigs? (Students should recognize how they stimulate her imagination. Ob called them *The Mysteries*, but they seemed to Summer to be physical representations of things difficult to interpret—thunderstorms, angels, fire, love, dreams, and even death.)

Writing

QUICK ASSESS

Do students' responses:

✔ give insights into the author's perspective?

✔ support these insights with evidence from the selection?

After writing about what Summer notices and values, students make inferences about Rylant's ideas, feelings, and values. Model an example, such as when Summer says that the trailer is a "paradise" because both May and Ob intended to make it an appealing home for a child. Help students to see this as a clue that Rylant valued the feeling of closeness in a family and believed in the importance of a loving environment for a child.

READING AND WRITING EXTENSIONS

➤ Read aloud Rylant's picture book, *When I Was Young in the Mountains*. Invite students to write their own childhood memoirs modeled after this short text. Suggest that they use the first four words of the title as their opening line or a repeating refrain.

➤ Invite students to make a sketch of what one of Ob's whirligigs looked like. Post students' creations on a bulletin board or wall for all to see.

See also Answer Key, page 116

Two Perspective and Style

Critical Reading

FOCUS

Cynthia Rylant's word choice, sentence patterns, and figurative language offer additional insight into her perspective as a writer.

BACKGROUND

"Perspective and Style" invites students to explore the language choices an author makes. Cynthia Rylant's style in *Missing May* was described in the *New York Times Book Review* as having the "spare language, sense of place, and deceptively simple stories" that make the novel "explode most effectively." Help students to recognize that Cynthia Rylant uses conversational speech patterns, detailed comparisons, and informal words. The language of the author can reveal much about the character's outlook. Rylant's years of living in West Virginia in poverty with her single mother offered a canvas for Summer's observations of May and Ob's trailer.

FOR DISCUSSION AND REFLECTION

➤ What words and phrases do you find vivid or striking? (Some students may point to the similies with which Summer describes herself: she is "like a homework assignment," "like one of those little mice who has to figure out the right button to push before its food will drop down into the cup.")

➤ Why did Summer state that she had "come home"? (She had always felt "caged and begging" when it came to food. The variety of food in May's kitchen—Oreos, Ruffles, Snickers, cardboard boxes of juice—delighted her.)

➤ Have there ever been times or places when eating was "a joy"? (Student responses will vary.)

Writing

QUICK ASSESS

Do students' explanations:

✔ show the connection between perspective and style?

✔ offer insight into Summer's perspective?

As a prewriting activity, students describe and analyze elements of Rylant's style. Then they are asked to explain whether that style helps or hinders the reader's ability to see the world from Summer's perspective.

READING AND WRITING EXTENSIONS

➤ Invite students to research the life of Cynthia Rylant. Suggest that they write the information they find in a question/answer interview format in which they are the interviewers and Rylant responds. Have pairs of students read the interviews to the class.

➤ Encourage students to write a scene for a one-act play based on the two excerpts from *Missing May*. Include a cast of characters, set design, and dialogue that imitates Rylant's informal style. Have classmates perform the scenes.

See also Answer Key, page 117

Three Perspective and Theme

Critical Reading

FOCUS

Cynthia Rylant describing her feelings about her writing:

"I get a lot of personal gratification thinking of those people who don't get attention in the world and making them really valuable in my fiction—making them absolutely shine with their beauty."

BACKGROUND

Cynthia Rylant has said of her protagonists, "I don't ever quite write happy novels; I don't want to deal with the people who have what they want. I want to deal with people who don't have what they want, to show their lives, too." In *The Soda Jerk*, Rylant portrays the people of a small town as they visit the soda fountain and are observed by the soda jerk, the teenage boy waiting on them at the counter. *The Soda Jerk* is a compilation of poetry written from the perspective of the teenager as he watches or retells an encounter with each customer.

➤ In "Sandy Jane Meador," Rylant presents the meeting between the most popular girl and the soda jerk. While he struggles to keep up with the conversation, the boy feels "so tired from all that work" and empty after Sandy Jane leaves.

FOR DISCUSSION AND REFLECTION

➤ How would you describe Sandy Jane? (Answers may include popular, a chatterbox, self-centered, smiling, and shallow.)

➤ Why does the Soda Jerk feel so tired? (It was a great effort to impress the girl. It wasn't a natural conversation because there was never a "hole," and he was trying so hard to make her like him.)

➤ How would you describe the speaker? (Students will say the boy is intimidated by Sandy Jane, nervous around her, and hopeful that she will like him.)

Writing

QUICK ASSESS

Do students' responses:

✓ illuminate the perspective of "an outsider looking in"?

✓ comment on the contrast between inner reality and outward appearances?

Have students discuss the difference between how the conversation might have appeared to anyone observing it and how the soda jerk actually felt. For example, another teenager might have been jealous that the popular girl was with the soda jerk while he actually was feeling inadequate throughout the meeting. This discussion could introduce the idea of inner reality vs. outward appearances and should help students to write about how this poem connects to Rylant's perspective of "an outsider looking in."

READING AND WRITING EXTENSIONS

➤ Encourage students to write the actual conversation between Sandy Jane Meador and the Soda Jerk.

➤ Invite students to read other selections from *The Soda Jerk*. Have them select one of their favorite poems to share aloud with the class.

See also Answer Key, page 117

Four Perspective in Autobiography

Critical Reading

FOCUS

Cynthia Rylant on her adolescence in Beaver, West Virginia:

"As long as I stayed in Beaver, I felt I was somebody important. I felt smart and pretty and fun. But as soon as I left town ... my sense of being somebody special evaporated into nothing and I became dull and ugly and poor."

BACKGROUND

In this passage from *But I'll Be Back Again,* a collection of autobiographical essays, Cynthia Rylant describes Beaver, West Virginia, the town to which she moved when she was eight. As an adult, Rylant has said that Beaver was "without a doubt a small, sparkling universe that gave me a lifetime's worth of material for my writing." But as an adolescent, she suffered great insecurity in Beaver; ashamed of her own poverty and looking beyond Beaver as a place of adventure. It "appeared backward and dull compared to larger cities." This lesson connects Rylant's own background and feeling as an outsider to the outlook that her characters often maintain as loners and observers.

FOR DISCUSSION AND REFLECTION

➤ What details does Rylant focus on in the description of her home? (Answers may include old gas heaters, old green and brown linoleum, spiders in the bathroom, a view of a warehouse and junkyard.)

➤ What is Rylant's attitude to her home? (Students should suggest that Rylant is ashamed of her home and reluctant to bring anyone there. Rylant envies Christy Sanders's home, described in great contrast to hers. She admits her desire for better things and her belief that the world would judge her "unworthy" because of where she lived.)

➤ Ask students to think about places where they might not want to go because they feel "so unequal" to the others they would see there.

Writing

QUICK ASSESS

Do students' responses:

✓ connect details about Rylant to her characters?

✓ explore her focus on outsiders?

After discussing Rylant's life in Beaver, ask students to refer to the earlier selections from *Missing May* and *The Soda Jerk.* Both Summer and the soda jerk have been established as outsiders, and thinking about them will help students to write about Rylant's own perspective.

READING AND WRITING EXTENSIONS

➤ Encourage students to read one of the many children's books from Rylant's *Henry and Mudge* series. Have them discuss the relationship developed between the young boy and his dog.

➤ Invite students to read from another of Rylant's novels, such as *A Blue-Eyed Daisy, A Fine White Dust,* or *I Had Seen Castles.* Have them report orally on what, if anything, they learned about Rylant's perspective.

See also Answer Key, page 117

Five Reflecting on Perspective

Critical Reading

FOCUS

Understanding how writers reflect on their experiences can give us clues about their perspectives.

BACKGROUND

Lesson Five returns to Rylant's autobiography, *But I'll Be Back Again,* and an account of a moment when her life changed. As she describes the symphony's visit to her junior high school in Beaver, the reader begins to see what sparked her to become a writer and learn more about the world. Her experience listening to the beautiful music made her no longer satisfied with Beaver (her "curse") and, at the same time, gave her the motivation to move beyond Beaver to become a writer, "her gift." In a *Horn Book* interview, Rylant described her writing as giving her "a sense of self-worth" that she didn't have during her whole childhood. "I am really proud," wrote Rylant, that books "have carried me through some troubled times and have made me feel that I am worthy of having a place on this earth."

FOR DISCUSSION AND REFLECTION

➤ How was the visit from the New Orleans Symphony Orchestra to her junior high school like "a visit from God Himself"? (The gym was transformed into a place of wonder—something she has never forgotten. Rylant had not been familiar with any sort of culture, and the experience opened up the world to her.)

➤ Why does Rylant imagine the conductor lives in a "pink house in New Orleans"? (Responses will vary. Students may find Rylant's description of his life quite amusing—the luxury of servants and a canopy bed and his friendship with such diverse singers as Elvis Presley, Paul McCartney, and The Monkees.)

Writing

QUICK ASSESS

Do students' journal entries:

✓ explain the significance of an experience?

✓ include their feelings at the time and their later reflections?

Before writing a journal entry about a significant childhood moment, have students generate topic ideas by brainstorming a list of the top best things that ever happened to them and then a list of the ten worst.

READING AND WRITING EXTENSIONS

➤ Have students imagine they are the symphony conductor. What might he have thought about the audience, the small town, or the music? Ask students to write a letter that the conductor might send to a friend in which he describes his feelings about the concert in Beaver.

➤ Encourage students to imagine that twenty-five years from now they have become famous and are asked to write a brief paragraph about where they grew up. Suggest that they describe one brief incident (as Rylant did with the concert) to help them focus their thoughts about their home towns and the people who live there.

THE READER'S RESPONSE

Unit Overview

This unit is designed to help students sharpen their ability to respond to literature. As they read an excerpt from an autobiography, a poem, and a short story, students will assess and evaluate the facts in a selection. Then they will learn how to move beyond a factual response to interpret what they read more effectively.

Literature Focus

	Lesson	Literature
1.	Factual Response	**Eleanor Roosevelt,** from *The Autobiography of Eleanor Roosevelt* (Autobiography)
2.	Interpretive Response	**Emily Dickinson,** "Because I could not stop for Death" (Poetry)
3.	Supporting Your Interpretation	
4.	Evaluative Response	**William Sleator,** "The Elevator" (Short Story)
5.	Connecting to Your Life	**William Sleator,** "The Elevator" (Short Story)

Reading Focus

1. One way that readers respond is by understanding the who, what, where, when, and how of what they read.
2. When you interpret, you make reasonable guesses about a selection's meaning.
3. Good readers build an interpretation by finding words or phrases from a selection to support their views.
4. When you make an evaluative response, you make a judgment about what you have read.
5. When you connect a story to your own life, the story usually becomes more meaningful to you as a reader.

Writing Focus

1. Write a brief profile using facts from an autobiography.
2. Write questions and answers based on your interpretation of a poem.
3. Agree or disagaree with a poet's view of death.
4. Evaluate the beginning of a short story.
5. Connect the events of a story to your personal experience.

One Factual Response

Critical Reading

FOCUS

A reader's response begins with understanding the facts:

"You must do the thing which you think you cannot."

BACKGROUND

An autobiography about a person's life comes under the category of literary nonfiction. One would read it not as a history text, but as a fictional story, only with real people as the characters. Eleanor Roosevelt is the narrator of her autobiography. Speaking from the first-person point of view, she provides the reader with facts about her life and insight about her personality. The autobiography gives the reader the opportunity to learn about Roosevelt's life and how she feels about significant experiences.

➤ Lesson One presents students with many facts about Eleanor Roosevelt (1884–1962). She was a woman of paradox, as she battled her personal sense of inadequacy as a wife and mother yet also personified strength and independence. She had deep compassion for those who suffered, and following her husband's death in 1945, Roosevelt was a champion of minority rights as a delegate to the United Nations. Many people believe that she is one of the most effective, if not *the* most effective, women ever in United States politics.

FOR DISCUSSION AND REFLECTION

➤ What are some of Eleanor Roosevelt's internal conflicts? (Her self-esteem was low; she felt ugly, unloved, and socially awkward.)

➤ What are some external conflicts that she dealt with? (She struggled to meet high expectations as a wife and mother and always put others first.)

➤ How did Eleanor's sense of duty affect her life? (She concentrated so much on what she thought others expected of her that she neglected her own personal life.)

➤ What do you think she learned about life in general? (Answers may vary, but they may include that it's important to lead a life that is full of love and caring for others but also to be true to yourself and face any challenge.)

Writing

QUICK ASSESS

Do students' profiles:

✓ include a variety of facts from the autobiography?

✓ offer a thoughtful description of Roosevelt?

Before students use the facts they listed to write a profile of Eleanor Roosevelt, it would be helpful to review with them some facts about F. D. R. and his presidential leadership to refresh students' memories about the time period—at home and globally—in which Eleanor Roosevelt lived.

READING AND WRITING EXTENSIONS

➤ Ask students to consider Eleanor Roosevelt's statement that "grief and . . . loneliness . . . are the lot of most human beings." Do they agree? Why or why not?

➤ Encourage students to work in small groups to use other biographies and the Internet to research more information about Eleanor Roosevelt. Then have them complete a compare-and-contrast poster of Eleanor Roosevelt and a more current First Lady.

See also Answer Key, page 117

Two Interpretive Response

Critical Reading

FOCUS
To interpret a text's meaning, active readers use authors' clues as the basis of inferences.

BACKGROUND
Many writers do not tell the readers everything they want them to know. Writers often expect readers to infer information, making logical guesses using the clues and hints in the writing. Inference is based on the challenge of using the information at hand to "read" the author's tone, understand the figurative language, and solve the author's "puzzle." Emily Dickinson invites the reader to move beyond the facts to interpret her poem "Because I could not stop for Death."

➤ Students will be challenged in this lesson to examine the poem, line by line, and to understand what it means and why Dickinson chose the form she did. For example, it's important that students think how the speaker of the poem—the "I"—might symbolize humans in general and how one's physical life is a journey that inevitably ends at "A Swelling of the Ground," or one's death. Help students understand that with "the Setting Sun," life comes to an end in death; yet the ending is happy as the "Horses' Heads" are pointed toward a spiritual life in "Eternity."

FOR DISCUSSION AND REFECTION
➤ What is Dickinson's tone when she uses the word "kindly" in line 2? (Students may say that it shows an attitude of sarcasm that "death" is being so accommodating.)

➤ Why do you think that the poet uses capital letters and dashes after particular words? (It seems Dickinson wants to emphasize certain things and is in no hurry to finish the carriage ride.)

➤ Can you find an example of alliteration? (Students may point to "Gazing Grain," "Setting Sun," "Gossamer, my Gown," or "Tippet—-only Tulle.")

Writing

QUICK ASSESS
Do students' responses:
✓ include four thoughtful questions?
✓ express reasonable answers?

Interpreting poetry is an activity that some students may find difficult. Use an overhead transparency, working through the poem line by line with the class, to model the process of paraphrasing, questioning, and answering. Then let students continue to work independently or with a partner to create their own responses to Dickinson's poem.

READING AND WRITING EXTENSIONS
➤ Have students investigate other poems about death and consider how the subject is handled by different poets. Have them share their findings with the class.

➤ Invite the students to create a collage that represents their impressions of Dickinson's poem. Suggest that they use photos, words, or original drawings.

See also Answer Key, page 117

Three Supporting Your Interpretation

Critical Reading

FOCUS

A reader's interpretation of stories and poems is a product of the mind, the heart, and the supporting evidence found in the selection.

BACKGROUND

Drawing a conclusion or inference from a piece of writing is like making a delightful discovery—just like the pleasure we derive from finding the answer to a problem or figuring out a word in a puzzle. In the poem, "Because I could not stop for Death," Emily Dickinson does not say that the poem is about life and death, but we can infer this from the line, "He kindly stopped for me— . . . ." She does not say that life is a series of events, but she uses the word "passed" to show the reader a movement through many different experiences. She does not say that we're never ready for this "trip," but hints that we are dressed inappropriately for the chill.

➤ As students read through the poem, they will learn to gather the author's clues and use them to substantiate their interpretations of what they read. It's important to realize that there may be more than one reasonable interpretation and that different clues may offer evidence for different ideas. That's what makes poetry so fascinating—there are no definitive answers or explanations.

FOR DISCUSSION AND REFLECTION

➤ What does the word "He" keep referring to in the poem? (The word "He" stands for death.)

➤ What can you infer from the reference to the "Horses' Heads"? (Answers may include that since they are facing "Eternity" they know the way to heaven and, thus, the speaker may end up in heaven after death.)

➤ What do you think of the poem's rhythm? (Some students may describe the steady, deliberate pace of the poem—with the many dashes—as like the slow gait of the horse.)

➤ How recently did the events described in the poem occur? (Dickinson's use of the phrase "Since then—'tis Centuries—" suggests that the speaker has been dead for hundreds of years.)

Writing

QUICK ASSESS

Do students' explanations:

✔ state their opinion on Dickinson's view of death?

✔ include specific text support?

After finding different pieces of support for the interpretation that death comes slowly and peacefully, students will explain how they feel about Dickinson's view of death.

READING AND WRITING EXTENSIONS

➤ Have students read another poem by Emily Dickinson and look for stylistic elements that both poems contain.

➤ Encourage students to write a journal entry about a time when something or someone surprised them.

Four Evaluative Response

Critical Reading

FOCUS

Active readers know how to make judgments about what they read.

BACKGROUND

William Sleator, born in 1945 in Maryland, had parents who always encouraged him to be his own person. He took music lessons, was drawn toward reading, and participated in many extracurricular activities. At Harvard, he majored in English and used his music expertise while working as a practice accompanist for the London Ballet Company. Sleator has won numerous awards for young adult novels, such as *Interstellar Pig, The Duplicate*, and *Strange Attractors*. He injects humor in his work, while trying to entertain his audience with endings that provoke the reader to think about other people's feelings.

➤ Students may feel as if they are on an elevator—out of control—as they race through the first part of Sleator's story. It is a good read from the very first spooky sentence, which hooks the reader into moving quickly to find out what happens. He uses words like "old" and "small" and "nervous" to clue the reader that something is out of the ordinary. Students may recall their own anxieties about unpleasant closed-in experiences as they read.

FOR DISCUSSION AND REFLECTION

➤ What will happen next? (Predictions will vary but push students to examine text specifics for clues.)

➤ What do you "see" on the elevator? (Sleator helps us picture a tiny, grungy elevator, with a single fluorescent light and a slow shuddering pace.)

➤ How do you "feel" on the elevator? (Some students may say they feel as Martin does—claustrophobic, self-conscious, and nervous.)

➤ What is so weird about the fat lady? (In addition to her odd, "piggish look," she stands with her back toward the door, gazing at Martin.)

Writing

QUICK ASSESS

Do students' responses:

✓ explain their opinion of the story?

✓ include two descriptive adjectives?

Once students have read the excerpt, discuss together their responses to the story. As they share their choices of adjectives, have them point out exactly what makes Sleator's writing so vivid in the reader's mind. See if they notice the use of similes such as his footsteps echoed "like slaps on the cement" or the numbers blinking as if "they might simply give up." Sleator's description also uses wonderful sensory details that pull the reader right into the story.

READING AND WRITING EXTENSIONS

➤ Have students imagine they are Martin. Ask them to imagine the conversation he would have with a friend at school about the incident. How would he desribe what happened in the elevator?

➤ Encourage students to make a storyboard of the action thus far, using quotes from the text as captions for their pictures.

Five Connecting to Your Life

Critical Reading

FOCUS

The joy of reading comes from making meaningful, personal connections to a story and its characters:

"And in the morning, when the elevator door opened, the fat lady was waiting for him."

BACKGROUND

The thrill of reading frequently comes from making personal connections to the material. Help students to see that when they quietly smile or cry at the end of a story, when they feel like they know the characters, or feel disappointed because they want the story to continue, they are making meaningful, personal connections to the text. Once students get caught up in a "good" story and make these connections, they will understand the essence of what reading is all about.

➢ William Sleator makes it easy for students to connect to his story "The Elevator." Almost everyone has had a moment in their lives that they can connect with a part of his story—the setting, the characters, or the mystery. It's the kind of story that makes one's heart beat a little faster. Students should identify with Martin, the building, the elevator experience, or the father-son relationship without much difficulty.

FOR DISCUSSION AND REFLECTION

➢ Have students discuss times when they have been frightened by someone or something, especially times when others dismissed their fears.

➢ What do you predict will happen next? (Predictions will vary but ask students to approach the predictions from a realistic point of view, using evidence from the story as support.)

➢ How would you describe Martin? (Answers will vary, but we know he's a twelve-year-old who lives with his father and has low self-esteem.)

Writing

QUICK ASSESS

Do students' responses:

✓ reflect a thoughtful reading of the story?

✓ make at least one personal connection to the story?

Before students write their personal responses to the story, brainstorm with the class some of their connections on the overhead or a chalkboard. This will spark more ideas and help those who can't think of anything to write about. Encourage students to use vivid verbs and sensory language in their responses.

READING AND WRITING EXTENSIONS

➢ Invite students to add a one-paragraph ending to the story that describes what the fat lady does after the elevator doors close.

➢ Have students draw character sketches of Martin and the fat lady. Suggest that they include accompanying captions from the story and display their creations around the room.

Unit Overview

In this unit, students will practice techniques that are useful in reading social studies materials. Highlighting, summarizing, taking notes, and working with graphics are all important techniques that encourage students to be actively involved in their reading and can be used for other kinds of nonfiction.

Literature Focus

	Lesson	Literature
1.	Highlighting	**Cabell Phillips,** from *The 1940s: Decade of Triumph and Trouble* (Nonfiction)
2.	Summing Up	
3.	Pulling It Together	**John Hersey,** from *Hiroshima* (Nonfiction-Social Studies)
4.	Reading the Visuals	from *World History* (Nonfiction-Social Studies)
5.	Patterns of Organization	from *World History* (Nonfiction-Social Studies)

Reading Focus

1. Highlighting helps you identify important information.
2. Summarizing what you read helps you understand and remember it.
3. As you read social studies materials, take notes to organize ideas and use visual organizers to clarify your thoughts.
4. Graphics are compact sources of facts and statistics. When you come across a graphic in your reading, take time to examine it.
5. Recognizing how writers organize their writing helps you understand and organize what you read.

Writing Focus

1. Use highlighted facts from two different excerpts to write a paragraph.
2. Write three quiz questions and answers that reflect the major points of a selection.
3. Fill in a graphic with notes taken during reading.
4. Create a graphic that expresses information from a bar graph.
5. Write a paragraph that summarizes a passage of nonfiction.

One Highlighting

C r i t i c a l R e a d i n g

FOCUS

Highlighting helps you recognize and remember important information.

BACKGROUND

This lesson introduces students to the process of highlighting the most significant points in nonfiction text. Help students realize that when they need to review material and study for tests, highlighting will help them distinguish which material to study. They can use the headings and subheadings of chapters to help them find the key information. Point out that too much highlighting negates the whole point of the technique and just makes the text messy and confusing.

➤ Students may know little about America in the 1940s. Explain that in the early 1940s, the nation was bouncing back from the Great Depression. Americans were just getting back on their feet, emotionally and economically, when the country entered World War II. Once again people had to "tighten their belts" and try to save money. Students will be surprised at the prices for goods and services then and at all of the conveniences that people did without that we now take for granted.

FOR DISCUSSION AND REFLECTION

➤ What facts from 1940 surprised you the most? (Students may say that they are amazed that there was no television or air conditioning and that prices were so low.)

➤ What surprised you the most about the time period after 1942? (Answers may include that no automobiles could be bought or that people had to wait in line to buy certain foods with food stamps.)

➤ Why do you think there were shortages? (After the bombing of Pearl Harbor, on December 7, 1941, many goods went to the soldiers, and manufacturers retooled their machinery in order to produce aircraft and weapons for the war.)

➤ Why were people encouraged to buy war bonds? (These government funds went to support the war effort.)

W r i t i n g

QUICK ASSESS

Do students' paragraphs:

✓ show a comparison between life in 1940 and life in 1942?

✓ use highlighted facts as support?

Suggest that students do their highlighting of the two selections in two different colors and then arrange the highlighted facts in a Venn diagram before trying to write a paragraph comparing life in 1940 to life in 1942.

READING AND WRITING EXTENSIONS

➤ Have students respond in their journals to a popular phrase of the time, "use it up, wear it out, make it do, and do without." Ask them to think about what modern conveniences they would find it hard to do without.

➤ Invite students to interview older family members or friends about their memories of life in the 1940s. Students might want to find out about sacrifices and shortages during this period.

See also Answer Key, page 118

Two Summing Up

C r i t i c a l   R e a d i n g

FOCUS
A brief summary will capture the main idea of social studies material.

BACKGROUND

Lesson Two helps students summarize what they read and encourages them to figure out the main idea the writer is expressing. Students will easily realize that the subject of Phillips's writing is about the time period in America just prior to and just after the start of World War II, but it may be harder for them to decide what is the one most important thing Phillips says about that time period.

➤ Students often struggle with the summarizing process, but suggesting that they keep their summaries brief should help them arrive at the major idea. If students need additional practice summarizing, you might have them write brief plot summaries of a short story they have read or a television show they have seen.

FOR DISCUSSION AND REFLECTION

➤ What is the subject of Phillips's text? (The topic is the impact of the country's economy on daily living.)

➤ Did it help you to have the main points highlighted in the text when you created your questions? (Ask students to be very specific in their descriptions of how highlighting did or didn't help them.)

➤ Why is it important to distinguish main ideas from less important details? (Answers will vary.)

W r i t i n g

QUICK ASSESS
Do students' quizzes:

✔ reflect the major points of the selection?

✔ include three questions and answers?

After students reread the two selections by Cabell Phillips, it would be good for them to work with partners to come up with questions and answers for their quiz. Once they have completed the questions, divide the class into two teams—one to ask and the other to answer the questions. At the end, summarize with students the most important points of the selection.

READING AND WRITING EXTENSIONS

➤ Encourage students to do research at the library or on the Internet to learn more about ration stamps, war bonds, or other aspects of life in the 1940s that interest them. Suggest that students share one or two of the most interesting facts in a short oral report.

➤ Suggest that students read other novels that deal with the World War II time period at home and abroad. Possibilities include *Summer of My German Soldier* by Bette Greene, *Number the Stars* by Lois Lowry, and *Under the Blood Red Sun* by Graham Salisbury. Have them prepare an oral summary of the plot to present in class.

See also Answer Key, page 118

Three Pulling It Together

Critical Reading

FOCUS

Taking notes as you read helps you to organize important ideas.

BACKGROUND

John Hersey, a novelist and journalist, was born in 1914 in China. At the age of three, he and his mother traveled on a two-year trip around the world, and in 1924, at the age of ten, Hersey left China and moved to the United States where he graduated from Yale University in 1936. He became a secretary for Sinclair Lewis and was a war correspondent for *Life* and *Time* magazines during World War II. His writing exemplifies a spare, sure style, and he was honored with the Pulitzer Prize in 1945 for his novel about Italy, *A Bell for Adano*. Other Hersey novels include *The Wall* (1950) about Poland under Nazi rule and *The Marmot Drive* (1953), an allegory. His nonfiction work, *Hiroshima*, is a model of objective and accurate reporting.

➤ In "Pulling It Together," students are asked to take notes about Mr. Tanimoto's experiences. Help them see that not only journalists, but also doctors, lawyers, scientists, engineers, and teachers must learn to take notes that are accurate and thorough. Students who learn to take good notes will have an advantage in their education, as they learn to highlight and record important facts and summarize the most important ideas.

FOR DISCUSSION AND REFLECTION

➤ Why was the population of Hiroshima reduced to 245,000 people? (Many had already been evacuated.)

➤ Why did Mr. Matsuo and Mr. Tanimoto have time to react? (Students will likely say because they were two miles from the center of the explosion.)

➤ Why did the sky grow darker and darker? (The mushroom cloud was covering the sky with dust and debris.)

➤ Why did the Japanese soldiers in the cave—but not Mr. Tanimoto—become injured? (Answers may vary, but students may say that perhaps it was just luck.)

Writing

QUICK ASSESS

Do students' responses:

✓ show understanding of the main idea?

✓ list supporting events in chronological order?

It might be helpful for students to work with a partner or a small group as they read the essay and take notes. Have them compare notes with one another to sharpen their reading abilities and to prepare them to complete the graphic.

READING AND WRITING EXTENSIONS

➤ Share the beautiful picture book *The Faithful Elephants*, by Yukio Tsuchiya, aloud with the class to bring a different point of view to the bombing in Hiroshima.

➤ Have students look at examples of artwork such as "The Persistence of Memory" by Salvidor Dali or "City at the Sea" by Helmut Kies. Have students use them as inspiration to write poems about the bombing of Hiroshima from Mr. Tanimoto's point of view.

See also Answer Key, page 119

Four Reading the Visuals

Critical Reading

FOCUS

A graphic can make complex information easier to understand.

BACKGROUND

Graphics in social studies texts are a welcome addition to pages of written information. They break up the monotony of print, and they often give extra facts and details that are interesting and invite the reader to interact with the text. Good graphics are like good maps; they have titles and keys and labels that help the reader decipher and locate the necessary data.

➤ In "Reading the Visuals," students have the opportunity to look closely at vertical bar graphs. It would be helpful to point out to the whole class the parts of the graph, where different information is found, and how it is labeled. At this time, ask students to brainstorm other styles of graphs and charts that could show the same information in a different format. For instance, students could use a pie chart, a horizontal bar graph, a line graph, a flow chart, a spreadsheet, or even a web. They may even create a totally original graphic. Whatever the final creation, enough information should be included, and all of it must be labeled neatly and accurately.

FOR DISCUSSION AND REFLECTION

➤ Explain the title, "Costs of World War II." (The title is referring to the price of the war in lives lost, architecture lost, and psychological effects, not dollars spent.)

➤ What is the most frightening aspect of the text information? (Responses will vary, but students may mention that totalitarian dictatorships could be so powerful as to wipe out such huge numbers of people.)

➤ How did World War II affect people? (Opinions on this broad question will vary, but some students may point out that many people vowed to prevent "such horror from ever happening again.")

Writing

QUICK ASSESS

Do students' graphics:

✓ contain information from the text and the bar graph?

✓ contain a title, a key, and labels?

When students get ready to create their own graphics, they will need to know exactly what information and style of presentation they want to use. Lots of rough draft work will help them get the neatness and accuracy needed for a good final draft. Remind them that a title, labels, and a key are all necessary components of a user-friendly graphic.

READING AND WRITING EXTENSIONS

➤ Have students work with their teachers to create different kinds of graphics that present statistics from a chapter in a social studies textbook.

➤ Invite students to work with a partner to research other wars, such as the Civil War, World War I, or the Vietnam War. Suggest that they construct a graphic to present the information they find. Encourage them to show and explain their graphics to the class.

See also Answer Key, page 119

Five Patterns of Organization

Critical Reading

FOCUS

Social studies material is often arranged in chronological order, by comparison and contrast, and by details that support a main idea.

BACKGROUND

The purpose of expository text is often to inform or to explain; however, much of it does both. The title and author's topic are the reader's first clue as to what the material is about. And more often than not, each paragraph will have its own main idea, expressed in a topic sentence. In addition to a topic sentence, many paragraphs in social studies materials will contain supporting details, such as examples, reasons, and facts.

➤ The topic of the textbook excerpt in this lesson is revealed in the title, "The Atomic Bomb." Each paragraph of the selection deals with different support information about that topic, and the author moves in chronological order. Instead of arranging the material chronologically, the supporting details could include presidential support, effect on Hiroshima, effect on Nagasaki, and influence on the end of the war. A different format gives students a new way to look at the material and interact with the text.

FOR DISCUSSION AND REFLECTION

➤ How long had World War II been going on before the bombing of Hiroshima? (The answer is several years. The United States entered the war in 1941.)

➤ How much time elapsed between the bomb on Hiroshima and the end of the war? (Only twenty-four days after the bomb was dropped, World War II was over.)

➤ What do you think of Truman's decision? (There will probably be disagreement. Some students may say that using the bomb, as drastic as it was, brought quick closure to the war, but others may consider the mass killing unjustified.)

Writing

QUICK ASSESS

Do students' paragraphs:

✓ identify the main idea?

✓ include supporting details from the selection?

You might want to have students mark the text with different color highlighters—one color for chronological information and a second color for main idea and supporting details. When they start to think of the main idea, have students say, "What is the most important thing the author is saying about the topic?" Then, to find the supporting details, have them say, "I know this is true because. . . ." and have them fill in the reasons with details from the text. Once they complete the graphic organizer, writing the summary paragraph should be easy.

READING AND WRITING EXTENSIONS

➤ Have students reread the passages by Cabell Phillips in Lesson One. Ask them to create a Venn diagram to compare and contrast information about life in 1940 with facts about life in 1942.

➤ Encourage students to bring in current events news articles. After they summarize the main idea and supporting details of the articles, suggest that they use a graphic organizer, such as the one on page 146, to present key information.

See also Answer Key, page 119

NARRATIVE NONFICTION

Unit   Overview

In this unit, students will examine the genre of narrative nonfiction and its blend of personal story set against a factual background. As they explore how the author's feelings and personality are allowed to weave through a fabric of facts, students will practice identifying main ideas, recognizing details, making inferences, and examining author's intent.

Literature   Focus

	Lesson	Literature
1.	Story *and* Facts	**Terry Egan, Stan Friedmann, and Mike Levine,** from *Good Guys of Baseball* (Nonfiction)
2.	What's the Big Idea?	**Christopher de Vinck,** "Power of the Powerless: A Brother's Lesson" (Nonfiction)
3.	Details, Details	
4.	Inferencing	**Livia Bitton-Jackson,** from *I Have Lived a Thousand Years* (Nonfiction-Social Studies)
5.	Author's Purpose	

Reading   Focus

1. When you read a piece of narrative nonfiction, watch carefully for the facts the author presents.
2. In narrative nonfiction, the main idea is usually implied. Once you find the main idea, you can begin to consider the message the author has for you.
3. Details are important because they help the reader visualize a scene and get involved in the writing.
4. Making inferences about a character helps you build a portrait of the person you are reading about.
5. In narrative nonfiction, writers often make a direct statement of their purpose. Once you understand the author's intent, you can understand the idea or message the author has for you.

Writing   Focus

1. Write a bio of an athlete using facts from a selection of narrative nonfiction.
2. Select a topic and main idea for your own narrative nonfiction piece.
3. Show the relationship between a narrative's main idea and its supporting details.
4. Write a personality profile using factual and inferential information.
5. Explain whether an author has achieved her intended purpose.

One Story *and* Facts

Critical Reading

FOCUS

Narrative nonfiction strikes a balance between facts and story:

"Even after he became a big-league All-Star, Mo never forgot the kids."

BACKGROUND

Narrative nonfiction is a creative, factual account that is more personal than a textbook or a scientific article, but not just a pure fiction story. It may be elegant and formal, or loosely constructed and informal, depending on the style and message of the writer. This genre has great audience appeal because it is interesting to learn facts in a story format that seems so personal; narrative nonfiction allows the reader to respond, remember, and connect.

➤ In Lesson One, students read an excellent example of narrative nonfiction, "The Promise." Before they realize it, students are not only enjoying a good story, but learning many facts about baseball star Mo Vaughn. After the first reading, they'll have the opportunity to comb the story for facts and discuss the story elements that make it fiction.

FOR DISCUSSION AND REFLECTION

➤ What kind of role model do you think Mo Vaughn was for young people? (He is living proof that it's important to work hard, never give up, and take time for others.)

➤ What feelings did you experience as you read this story? (Answers will vary, but they may include surprise at Mo's determination, happiness that he made Jason so happy, and amazement at all he does for kids.)

➤ Why do the authors describe Mo by saying that he "floats silently" around the bases after the home run? (He was happy and relieved, having fulfilled his promise to the sick boy. His spirit was light, and his running seemingly effortless.)

Writing

QUICK ASSESS

Do students' responses:

✔ use enough facts from the story?

✔ convey a sense of Mo Vaughn?

Prior to reading the story, have students brainstorm ideas about the title and predict what they think the story might be about. Invite them to discuss one another's trading cards before students begin to write a brief bio of Mo Vaughn.

READING AND WRITING EXTENSIONS

➤ Have students read Rogelio R. Gomez's narrative nonfiction story "Foul Shots" or Bob Greene's "Baseball and the Facts of Life." Ask students to compare the story elements of those works with those in "The Promise."

➤ Encourage students to write a letter to Mo Vaughn, following the game in California, from Jason's point of view. Remind them to use the vocabulary and sentence structure of a young boy.

See also Answer Key, page 119

Two What's the Big Idea?

C r i t i c a l   R e a d i n g

FOCUS

Recognizing the main idea helps you understand what a piece of writing is all about:

"Oliver still remains the weakest, most helpless human being I ever met, and yet he was one of the most powerful human beings I ever met."

BACKGROUND

As they read narrative nonfiction, students need to sift through the facts and the details to identify the writer's main idea. Why is he or she writing? Help students to consider possible insights that the author wants to share with them. Usually the main idea is not stated directly in narrative nonfiction; thus, the reader needs to make inferences, or educated guesses, about what the writer is trying to communicate.

➤ In this lesson, students will read Christopher de Vinck's account of his brother Oliver. Ask them to think about what de Vinck is implying about Oliver. It is important that they realize the main idea can be stated in more than one way, and that, after they jot down several statements, they may decide that one is better than another. Remind students that they will need to identify the facts in the story that support their statements.

FOR DISCUSSION AND REFLECTION

➤ What was the probable cause of Oliver's brain damage? (Oliver's mother was overcome with fumes from a coal-burning stove when she was pregnant.)

➤ What are some clues that lead you to the main idea of the story? (Clues include how the author and his parents cared for Oliver, how they took him home and "loved" him and "liked" him, that they gave him gifts at Christmas and had him baptized.)

➤ What is so likable about de Vinck's narrative? (Answers may include that it mixes facts about Oliver's disabilities with a dash of humor and compassion for how he was treated by a remarkable, loving family.)

➤ What is Oliver's "power"? (Responses will vary. Students may note that even though he was disabled, Oliver was a source of love for the family who rose to the challenge of his care.)

W r i t i n g

QUICK ASSESS

Do students' responses:

✓ identify possible essay topics?

✓ state a main idea for a personal essay?

Before students plan their own narrative nonfiction accounts, they would benefit by hearing de Vinck's piece read aloud and then rereading it silently as they think about the main idea. It may be stated in more than one way, so have them listen carefully to their classmates' answers.

READING AND WRITING EXTENSIONS

➤ Encourage students to read from Christopher de Vinck's other books, such as his ***Only the Heart Knows How to Find Them*** and ***Songs of Innocence and Experience***. Have them explain whether or not they like his writing style and choice of topics.

➤ Have students write journal entries from different characters' points of view in this story—the mother, Roe, or the doctor at the hospital—and share them in small groups.

See also Answer Key, page 120

Five Author's Purpose

Critical Reading

FOCUS

In order to understand the author's intent, you must understand the author's message:

"My story is my message: Never give up."

BACKGROUND

Livia Bitton-Jackson was born in Bratislava, Czechoslovakia. During the last year of the war, when she was thirteen, she was taken to Auschwitz. The title of her memoir comes from an incident that occurred while Jews were being taken off the train. Apparently, a German woman came up to Bitton-Jackson and expressed her terror at the fact that "such old women were forced to work." It turned out that the woman was convinced that the teenager was a 65-year-old woman. Bitton-Jackson thought, "So this is liberation. It's come . . . . I am fourteen years old, and I have lived a thousand years . . . ."

➤ In this lesson, students will learn why Bitton-Jackson wrote the piece. Bitton-Jackson discusses her purpose by telling us that we must learn from the mistakes of the past. She is trying, as did Martin Luther King and Robert Kennedy, to evoke a commitment against prejudice and intolerance. She feels that awareness of the past will help prevent another similar catastrophe in the future. Help students to see that as the battle against prejudice and hatred continues, Bitton-Jackson's enduring message is never to give up.

FOR DISCUSSION AND REFLECTION

➤ Do you think Bitton-Jackson approves of movies such as *Schindler's List*? (Responses will vary. Students may infer from her reference to "sensational subjects on the silver screen" that she feels movies tend to fictionalize the truth; information should come from personal, first-hand survivor accounts.)

➤ Why does the author repeat certain words and phrases such as "my hope" and "lesson" and "never give up"? (It's her way of emphasizing how important it is for generations to come to know the truth about what happened in the Holocaust.)

Writing

QUICK ASSESS

Do students' responses:

✓ show understanding of Bitton-Jackson's purpose?

✓ explain whether or not she's achieved her purpose?

Before students begin writing, it would be helpful for them to reread the selection and share their ideas about the author's purpose with one another, so that many options have been listed on the overhead or chalkboard. Make sure that students use details from the selection to support their opinion on whether or not Bitton-Jackson has achieved her purpose.

READING AND WRITING EXTENSIONS

➤ Invite students to listen to music from the Holocaust, perhaps "Terezin: The Music 1941–44" (CD of music composed by prisoners in the Terezin concentration camp and smuggled out; on Romantic Robot label, London, 1991). Ask them to describe the mood it conveys.

➤ Read to students a children's picture book about the Holocaust, perhaps *The Children We Remember*, by Chana Byers Abells, or *Let the Celebration Begin*, by Margaret Wild. Encourage them to discuss what the author's purpose might have been.

See also Answer Key, page 120

U n i t   O v e r v i e w

This unit invites students to explore the style and the structure of the writings they read. Students will gain practice analyzing how an author chooses words and how he or she arranges them into sentences. As students examine several prose and poetry selections in this unit, they will become more aware of how authors mesh their writing style with different structures to create an engaging piece of literature.

L i t e r a t u r e   F o c u s

	Lesson	Literature
1.	Style Choices	**John Steinbeck,** from *The Pearl* (Fiction) **Judith Ortiz Cofer,** from "The Story of My Body" (Short Story)
2.	More Style Choices	
3.	The Structure	**Joyce Hansen,** from *I Thought My Soul Would Rise and Fly* (Fiction)
4.	Poetic Structure	**E. E. Cummings,** "l(a" (Poetry) **Diana Chang,** "Saying Yes" (Poetry)
5.	Structure *and* Style	

R e a d i n g   F o c u s

1. As you read, keep an eye on the author's word choices. Word choice makes an important contribution to style.
2. Writers make many different choices when it comes to style, including sentence length, dialogue, description, use of figurative language, and tone.
3. A writer can use structure to help readers connect with a story.
4. When you read a poem, note its structure. Poets sometimes use structure to help reveal their meaning.
5. Before you evaluate style and structure, first decide on criteria to use for the evaluation.

W r i t i n g   F o c u s

1. Use a Venn diagram to compare the word choices of two authors.
2. Explain the differences between two authors' styles..
3. Explain how structure affects your understanding of and interest in a story.
4. Explain a poem's meaning and comment on its structure.
5. Evaluate the style and structure of selections according to criteria you have developed.

One Style Choices

Critical Reading

FOCUS

Authors choose words carefully to produce specific feelings in readers:

"His teeth were bared and fury flared in his eyes and the Song of the Enemy roared in his ears."

BACKGROUND

Born in 1902 in the Salinas Valley of California, John Steinbeck worked at various odd jobs such as a fruit picker, a bricklayer, a ranch hand, and a reporter, before achieving any success as a writer. These jobs afforded him the opportunity to gain first-hand knowledge about the common man, and his sympathy for the underprivileged migrant workers surfaced in his novel *The Grapes of Wrath*, which won the Pulitzer Prize in 1940. The characters in *The Pearl*, published in 1947, are symbols for all who are victims of oppression and exploited by society. Other of Steinbeck's works include *Of Mice and Men* and *The Red Pony* (1937), *East of Eden* (1952), and *Travels with Charley in Search of America* (1962). Steinbeck won the Nobel Prize for Literature in 1962 and died in 1968.

➤ In "Style Choices," students will have the opportunity to critique the word choices that make Steinbeck's style distinctive and compare it to the writing of Judith Ortiz Cofer, a much younger poet and novelist. Born in Puerto Rico in 1952, Cofer grew up in two different worlds—enjoying her grandmother's stories in her first language, Spanish, and then moving back and forth between Puerto Rico and New Jersey for a twenty-year cycle. Her writing explores the tensions that can arise in the clash of two different cultures. Cofer has written two books of poetry and a collection of short stories. Her collection of essays and poems, *Silent Dancing: A Partial Remembrance of a Puerto Rican Childhood*, has received numerous awards and honors.

FOR DISCUSSION AND REFLECTION

➤ What does the music in Steinbeck's selection represent? (The music and songs represent the characters' moods or consciences and introduce conflicts in the story, as when the scorpion strikes and Kino hears "the Song of the Enemy.")

➤ Is there humor in Cofer's writing? (Responses may include phrases such as "born a white girl in Puerto Rico, but became a brown girl when I came to live in the United States," "classmates called me Skinny Bones," or "I learned to be invisible.")

Writing

QUICK ASSESS

Do students' Venn diagrams:

✓ describe key differences in word choice?

✓ describe similarities in word choice?

Before students compare the two writing styles in a Venn diagram, it would be helpful to review what *formal* and *informal* mean when describing an author's language.

READING AND WRITING EXTENSIONS

➤ Encourage students to read more of *The Pearl* or part of another Steinbeck work. In a paragraph, have them explain their impressions of his style.

➤ Invite students to make a sketch based on the sensory details Steinbeck or Cofer uses in his or her writing. Suggest that they title their works.

See also Answer Key, page 120

TWO More Style Choices

Critical Reading

FOCUS
Authors' styles are reflected in their choices of sentence length, vocabulary, dialogue, description, and tone.

BACKGROUND
The best advice often given to aspiring young writers is to read, read, and read. Help students understand that they shouldn't read just to copy someone else's style but to learn from good models. Just as a painter goes to a museum to study and sketch the paintings of the masters, writers should read and study the best work in their field of interest—to practice their craft and to develop their own individual style.

➤ Lesson Two continues the discussion of style, extending it to choices about sentence length, amount of description and dialogue, figurative language, and tone. Remind students that writers' decisions are often determined by their analysis of their intended audience.

FOR DISCUSSION AND REFLECTION
➤ Why do you think Steinbeck's work is more formal than that of Cofer? (Answers may include that he wrote in an earlier time period and liked to use vivid, figurative language. Much of Cofer's writing has been inspired from more recent personal experience, and the subject matter affects the tone.)

➤ How does writing in the first person affect the style? (Students may say that it helps make writing informal and personal, while it warms up the tone.)

➤ From what point of view does Steinbeck tell *The Pearl?* (It is third-person, omniscient.)

➤ Do you prefer Steinbeck's or Cofer's style? Why? (Responses will vary.)

Writing

QUICK ASSESS
Do students' responses:

✓ describe differences between Steinbeck's and Cofer's styles?

✓ include specific information from their charts?

✓ explain how each writer's style matches the subject?

Once students examine Steinbeck's and Cofer's works closely enough to fill in the grid, they will be able to describe the key differences in their styles. Encourage students to go through the excerpts line by line, to think about why they like a particular style, and to consider why authors make particular style choices.

READING AND WRITING EXTENSIONS
➤ Have students continue *The Pearl* by adding an additional paragraph. Suggest that they try to imitate Steinbeck's style and vocabulary.

➤ Ask students to write a brief narrative, beginning with a version of Cofer's first sentence: "I was born _____ but became _____."

Three The Structure

Critical Reading

FOCUS

The structure of a piece of writing can offer clues to its meaning.

BACKGROUND

Authors make continuous decisions about how to structure their writing, from the lead that "hooks" the reader all the way through to the conclusion. In the excerpt from her novel presented in Lesson Three, a letter, Joyce Hansen makes a first-person account so vivid that readers feel as if they are listening to the characters themselves. She combines events and circumstances from original source material with fictional characters and a dash of humor to reveal little-known information about black soldiers' participation in the Civil War. Hansen teaches and lives in New York City and is the winner of the Coretta Scott King Award for *Which Way to Freedom* and its sequel, *Out From This Place*.

➤ Hansen's lead grabs the readers' attention with the very first sentence. She puts questions in the readers' mind, and they are eager to find out the answers. Who is speaking? What's going to happen to everyone, young and old? Why is this happening?

FOR DISCUSSION AND REFLECTION

➤ What did you learn about Patsy from this letter? (Students may say that she is a young, freed slave, has a great yearning to go to school, and feels no bitterness toward whites or "Yankees.")

➤ What kinds of chores were done by the slaves? (Answers should include sweeping, picking cotton in the fields, working in the gardens and orchards, cleaning in the house, and so on.)

➤ Where is the climax? (Students may say the climax occurs when Brother Solomon asks for a school.)

➤ What does "we all in this cauldron together" mean? (Students' answers should stress that everyone is part of a group that will look out for each other.)

Writing

QUICK ASSESS

Do students' responses:

✓ show an understanding of the author's structure?

✓ discuss changes in Patsy?

Before they write about the character of Patsy, encourage students to use a plot diagram to mark the structure of the letter. Thinking about the different parts of the story along with the dialogue and dialect should lead students to realize how effectively Hansen has blended historical events and fictional characters.

READING AND WRITING EXTENSIONS

➤ Encourage students to read and discuss in small groups various picture books about the Civil War. Possibilities include *Follow the Drinking Gourd*, by Jeanette Winter; *Minty: A Story of Young Harriet Tubman*, by Alan Schroeder and Jerry Pinkney; and *Nettie's Trip South*, by Ann Turner.

➤ Invite students to describe the structure of a poem or short story that they like. Ask them to think about why the author organized the work the way he or she did.

See also Answer Key, page 121

Four Poetic Structure

Critical Reading

FOCUS

Poets choose structures that best suit the meanings and feelings they are trying to communicate.

BACKGROUND

In "Poetic Structure," students will begin to recognize that like a musician's score, the poet's final product is a combination of many "instruments"—background, meaning, structure, and style. This lesson is designed to deepen students' understanding of poetic structure and to sharpen their ability to respond to poetry.

➤ E. E. Cummings (1894–1962), a Harvard graduate, is noted for his eccentricities of language, punctuation, and typography. The unique style and structure of his poetry shout to the reader, "Be yourself; be an individual." He prized this message more than any other; "it's you—nobody else—who determine your destiny and decide your fate." In addition to books, Cummings wrote plays and volumes of poetry. Diana Chang, born into a literary family, is a charter member of the International Society of Poets and winner of the Editors' Choice Award. Her poems differ in structure from those of Cummings and convey a somewhat different message. In "Saying Yes," she celebrates her Chinese heritage and expresses pride in her ethnic background.

FOR DISCUSSION AND REFLECTION

➤ How do the poems' structures reveal their messages? (Encourage students to be creative in their responses. Students should see how Cummings's vertical row arrangement of single syllables and letters imitates the action of a single falling leaf, solitary and alone, perhaps like the feelings of a person who marches to his or her own drum. Chang's poem uses a combination of twos to reveal the speaker's pride in a dual ethnic background; couplets, double repetitions, using the word "twice" and "both," and so on.)

➤ Why do you think Chang used a dialogue format to voice her message? (Answers may vary, but it's another way to strengthen the feeling of two—back and forth questions and answers to express a thought.)

Writing

QUICK ASSESS

Do students' responses:

✓ show understanding of the structure of Chang's stanzas?

✓ explain the poem's meaning?

A starting point for writing about the structure and meanings of the two poems is to read them aloud and recognize the poems' "single" vs. "double" formats.

READING AND WRITING EXTENSIONS

➤ Invite students to use the Cummings and Chang poems as models as they compose poems of their own that give a visual and verbal message.

➤ Have students select a phrase or image from one of the poems in this unit and create a drawing or sketch to represent it. Suggest that they use a line from a favorite song as a title.

See also Answer Key, pages 121–122

Five Structure *and* Style

Critical Reading

FOCUS
Evaluation of style and structure is based on a particular set of criteria chosen by the reader.

BACKGROUND
Lesson Five provides students with an opportunity to evaluate selections based on chosen criteria. They can brainstorm ideas for their list with classmates as well as peruse the lessons for hints of evaluation standards. For example, under "Style," they might include such elements as word choice, sensory or figurative language, and level of formality. They may also include sentence length, dialogue, and description.

➤ When people say, "It was a good book" or "That movie was good," what do they really mean? Remind students that they can't be sure of an evaluation's meaning until they know what *good* means. Critical readers should be able to list different criteria that constitute an evaluation. Seeing these criteria in the form of a chart or "rubric" allows students to provide a basis for their judgments.

FOR DISCUSSION AND REFLECTION
➤ What items could you include for criteria for style? (Style may include metaphors, similes, personification, rhythm, rhyme, alliteration, word choices, sentence length, dialogue, and tone.)

➤ What items could you include as criteria of structure? (Structure should include effective choice of genre, organization, repetition, interesting presentation of facts and message, and personal connection to the reader.)

Writing

QUICK ASSESS
Do students' charts:

✓ include important criteria under the categories of style and structure?

✓ cover all the selections in the unit?

Let students gather criteria for their rubrics working in pairs and then have them decide on the format for rating the different criteria as a whole class. For example, they could use categories of Excellent—Average—Poor or a continuum of points from 1—10. Remind students to keep the criteria general enough so that the rubric could be used for any literature selections, not just the ones in their book. Encourage students to be creative with the scoring descriptors, using such gradations as "Good—knocks my socks off!" or "Okay, nothing to write home about," or "What a snooze!"

READING AND WRITING EXTENSIONS
➤ Have students select a kind of book they enjoy reading—perhaps mystery, science fiction, or biography. Ask them to develop a list of three criteria they would use to judge a book of that type good.

➤ Invite students to use their criteria to evaluate another poem. Have them check to see if their list of criteria needs any adjustments, additions, or deletions.

See also Answer Key, page 122

POETIC FORMS AND TECHNIQUES

Unit Overview

This unit invites students to explore a variety of poetic structures and techniques and to consider why and how poets make choices about what form, rhythm, and rhyme to use. As they read and examine the writings of Emily Dickinson, Walt Whitman, William Shakespeare, Richard Wright, and Edgar Lee Masters, students will consider how traditional sonnets and haiku follow precise rules for construction, whereas free verse poems break all the rules.

Literature Focus

	Lesson	Literature
1.	Breaking the Rules	**Emily Dickinson,** "I'm Nobody" (Poetry)
2.	Patterns of Sound	**Walt Whitman,** "O Captain! My Captain!" (Poetry)
3.	The Sonnet	**William Shakespeare,** from *Romeo and Juliet,* (Drama)
4.	Haiku	**Richard Wright,** "Four Haiku" (Poetry)
5.	Free Verse	**Edgar Lee Masters,** "Hannah Armstrong" (Poetry)

Reading Focus

1. Poets sometimes choose punctuation that is unconventional to emphasize a point. When you see that happen in a poem, try to figure out why the poet wrote the poem that way.

2. Poets use sound patterns to emphasize certain points and to create an overall feeling that cannot always be created through prose writing.

3. A sonnet is a traditional form for a poem. When you read a sonnet, try to figure out why the poet chose that form to express his or her ideas.

4. Poets use haiku to express ideas simply and compactly. When you are reading haiku, try to figure out what the poet wants to reveal about the subject of the poem by expressing ideas in this way.

5. Poets can use free verse to express their thoughts without using set patterns of rhyme or rhythm.

Writing Focus

1. Explain an author's use of punctuation.

2. Write a news article using factual information in a poem and evaluate the effectiveness of the two forms.

3. Explore reasons why a poet might choose the traditional sonnet as a poetic form.

4. List advantages and disadvantages of using the poetic form of haiku.

5. Create a graphic that illustrates similarities and differences among sonnets, haiku, and free verse and use it to discuss why free verse is considered poetry.

One Breaking the Rules

Critical Reading

FOCUS

Some writers, such as Emily Dickinson, use unconventional punctuation that doesn't always follow the rules:

"How dreary—to be—Somebody!"

BACKGROUND

"Breaking the Rules" should interest students who have often grown up being taught to do everything "by the rules." When students learn that it's okay to "break the rules," they often have a keen interest in the topic. One poet who broke the rules was Emily Dickinson. Her unconventional use of punctuation and structure is only a small indication of the reclusive and unorthodox life that she led. Always dressed in white, she spent most of her life (1830–1886) on the second floor of her family home in Amherst, Massachusetts, keeping her nearly 1800 poems a secret, even from her family.

➤ The short lyric poem "I'm Nobody" expresses the thoughts of a single speaker, echoing, perhaps, Dickinson's personal philosophy about leading a quiet, introspective life. It's important to point out to the students that in the first stanza the poet uses question marks that almost force a whisper from the reader, while in the second stanza, the hyphens and exclamation points encourage volume and boasting, imitating the bullfrog's repetitious sound. The capitalization helps emphasize that a "Nobody" can be just as important as a "Somebody."

FOR DISCUSSION AND REFLECTION

➤ Why do you think Emily Dickinson would write about being a "nobody"? (Answers may vary. She seemed to prefer a quiet, secretive life without fanfare or fame. Her volumes of writing weren't published until four years after her death.)

➤ Discuss the poem's title, "I'm Nobody." (Students should see the irony. Emily Dickinson is considered one of the most important influences on modern poetry today, very much a "somebody.")

➤ Who is the "admiring Bog"? (It is the public eye, the fans, the general community or society.)

➤ What is the meaning of the poem? (She may be saying that people shouldn't need an audience or approval of others, that they are individuals and should satisfy themselves.)

Writing

QUICK ASSESS

Do students' responses:

✓ show understanding of the poem's meaning?

✓ comment on the unconventional punctuation?

Before writing about the poem's meaning, students should take turns reading the poem aloud; if they experiment with different oral interpretations, they will locate the departures from conventional punctuation usage more easily.

READING AND WRITING EXTENSIONS

➤ Have students write a poem using a copy of Andrew Wyeth's painting "Christina's World" as inspiration. Suggest that they use unconventional punctuation to help emphasize their message and feelings.

➤ Suggest that students work in small groups to learn more about Emily Dickinson's life and her work. Have them read other poems and share their findings and impressions with the class.

See also Answer Key, page 122

Two Patterns of Sound

Critical Reading

FOCUS

Sound patterns in poetry help emphasize mood and overall effect:

"O Captain! my Captain! rise up and hear the bells; / Rise up—for you the flag is flung—for you the bugle trills ...."

BACKGROUND

Reading poetry to yourself is like watching television with the sound turned off. In order to gain the full effect, poetry must be an audio experience. In some ways, poets are like the sound technicians at a rock concert who pump up the volume; without the audio portion, the whole effect is diminished or even lost. Walt Whitman's grief stricken response in "O Captain! My Captain!" to President Lincoln's death in 1865 uses an extended metaphor of a ship who has lost its captain. Whitman had worked as a nurse in military hospitals during the Civil War in Washington, D.C., and, as an American who loved democracy, he eulogized the loss of a great president.

➤ Whitman uses sound patterns masterfully, employing the techniques and patterns of rhythm, rhyme, repetition, and alliteration to express meaning and feelings to the reader. By reading aloud from "O Captain! My Captain!" students will feel the stately rhythm that simulates the pomp and allegiance of the ceremonies surrounding a fallen leader. Whitman uses internal rhyme in the middle of lines ("The port is near, the bells I hear ....") and end rhyme in the ends of lines ("done" and "won") that, along with repetition and alliteration, help to emphasize the somber mood of the poem.

FOR DISCUSSION AND REFLECTION

➤ How does the poem make you feel? (Students may answer that phrases such as "grim and daring," "bleeding drops of red," and "Fallen cold and dead" create a somber tone, making the reader feel sad and depressed.)

➤ Why did Whitman use the metaphor of a ship to eulogize President Lincoln? (Students may say that Lincoln was a great leader who guided the country during the Civil War, just as a captain steers his ship through a huge storm.)

Writing

QUICK ASSESS

Do students' writings:

✓ use factual information in their news articles?

✓ compare the effectiveness of the poem and the article?

Once students have examined the different sound techniques and thought about why they are used, it would be helpful for them to go back through the poem marking factual information with a different color highlighter. These facts, along with any prior knowledge they may have, will help them write an accurate news article. They'll probably realize that the poem is capable of conveying a more emotional message than their article.

READING AND WRITING EXTENSIONS

➤ Invite students to select appropriate music for background accompaniment while they recite the poem to the class live or on videotape.

➤ Ask students to write a poem in honor of someone that they admire who has died. Encourage them to emulate Whitman's use of sound techniques and repetition.

Three The Sonnet

Critical Reading

FOCUS

Sonnets are the songs of the ages, natural and timeless:

"Saints do not move, though grant for prayers' sake. / Then move not, while my prayer's effect I take."

BACKGROUND

This lesson is a challenging look at a sonnet's construction and the reasons for its use. As students work with the language of *quatrains* and *couplets*, they will also learn how to note the rhyme scheme of each quatrain. It will be helpful to work through each line together to make sure that students continue to note each new rhyming sound with additional letters of the alphabet, repeating the letters for already introduced sounds. (For instance, the first two quatrains would be *abab cbcb*.)

➤ Students may be interested to know that Shakespeare's genius (unlike that of Emily Dickinson) was recognized in his own time. Born in 1564 in Stratford-Upon-Avon, England, he was a prolific writer of plays and poems. Shakespeare's 154 sonnets, published in 1609, show Elizabethan qualities of originality, melody, and rhythm that may reveal secrets from his own life; they are the "songs" of his plays written for ordinary people. Shakespeare used the meter of unrhymed iambic pentameter, which was swift and noble, yet rhythmic and natural.

FOR DISCUSSION AND REFLECTION

➤ Why does the meter of the poem include variations? (Students may say that if the meter were exactly the same throughout, it would become mechanical, monotonous, and boring.)

➤ Why might Shakespeare have used the sonnet in his plays? (As students consider this question, point out that during the performance these lyrics would be sung by the actors, who were also skilled singers. It made the play more entertaining and added another dimension to the main characters.)

➤ What are Romeo and Juliet "doing" in this sonnet? (They are flirting with each other, just as young people would today, having met at a party or a dance.)

➤ Do you find this sonnet difficult to read? (Students' answers will vary.)

Writing

QUICK ASSESS

Do students' responses:

✔ show understanding of Shakespeare's sonnet?

✔ give thoughtful reasons for using the sonnet form?

As you begin this lesson, explain to students that the organization of a Shakespearean sonnet poses a question or problem that is resolved in the final couplet. Discussion of the sonnet will help students to write about reasons a poet might choose to use this traditional form.

READING AND WRITING EXTENSIONS

➤ Bring in examples of Elizabethan music to share with the class to enhance their understanding of this time period. With this music as a background, have students act out the sonnet and other lines from the play *Romeo and Juliet*.

➤ Suggest that students write an original sonnet, following Shakespeare's model, but using '90s language.

See also Answer Key, page 123

Four Haiku

Critical Reading

FOCUS

Haiku verses express feelings simply and compactly:

"Standing in the field,
I hear the whispering of
Snowflake to snowflake."

BACKGROUND

Richard Wright (1908–1960) is perhaps known best for his autobiography, *Black Boy*. He experienced a difficult childhood, plagued by his mother's illness and other family problems. Wright learned to read long before he entered school and used books as an escape; he left home at the age of fifteen and set off on his own. His books are what sustained him, and he's now recognized as one of the important American writers of the twentieth century. Wright's writing is noted for its use of vivid images and figurative language that help the reader to see ordinary things in a new perspective.

➤ In Lesson Four, students read and respond to Wright's "Four Haiku." These seventeen-syllable structures, arranged in three lines of 5-7-5 syllable order, originated in Japan in the latter part of the sixteenth century. Deceptively simple, yet beautiful and fleeting in their honesty and attention to detail, haiku are nature's "snapshots." The poet usually describes a fleeting moment found in nature, something very moving that he or she has observed.

FOR DISCUSSION AND REFLECTION

➤ What is Richard Wright's "Four Haiku" about? (Responses will vary. He has captured in just twelve lines the four seasons; then on a deeper level, he has expressed a person's movement through the life cycle, from childhood to adulthood.)

➤ What sensory description do you like? (Responses may include sensory descriptions such as "balmy spring," "green cockleburrs," "whispering of / Snowflake to snowflake.")

➤ Why do you think Wright wrote haiku rather than prose? (Answers will vary, but possibly Wright wanted to communicate impressions and mystery, the challenge of saying more with less.)

Writing

QUICK ASSESS

Do students' responses:

✓ show understanding of the haiku structure?

✓ identify advantages and disadvantages to using this form?

Before they write about poetic form, allow students to brainstorm ideas from nature that they might wish to capture in an original haiku. Try to move them beyond the overused subjects of rainbows and fluffy clouds. It would be helpful to share the work of Basho and Moritake as examples.

READING AND WRITING EXTENSIONS

➤ Have students illustrate at least one of their haiku verses and then create a class collection of student works to display in the school library.

➤ Ask students to write a journal entry reflecting on the statement "Less is more," based on their experience writing haiku.

Five Free Verse

Critical Reading

FOCUS

Free verse poetry often sounds natural and conversational:

"I wrote him a letter asking him for old times' sake

To discharge my sick boy from the army ...."

BACKGROUND

Free verse is poetry that doesn't follow a set form; it is "free" of meter and rhyme. It uses pauses and rhythm in its attempt to sound conversational and natural. Edgar Lee Masters (1868–1950), who grew up in Lewistown, Illinois, is most famous for his *Spoon River Anthology*, published as a serial version in 1914–1915. In it, he combined the experiences of former residents of Lewistown with his own childhood experiences. This original and provocative work has been compared to Walt Whitman's *Leaves of Grass* in its literary significance. Masters's work stands in strong contrast to the sentimental trends of the time.

➤ In this lesson, students have the opportunity to read and comment on Masters's poem "Hannah Armstrong." It portrays a poignant relationship between Aunt Hannah and Abe Lincoln. The conversational tone and repeated use of the pronoun "he" and "him" build in some mystery, and the style is personal and conversational.

FOR DISCUSSION AND REFLECTION

➤ What does "I boarded him" mean? (It means that the speaker rented out a room to Abraham Lincoln before he was famous.)

➤ What does the poem suggest about Abe Lincoln? (Students may note that it tells readers that Abe remembers his roots and is loyal to old acquaintances.)

➤ Do you find the poem convincing? (Students may note that although there is no rhyme, there is a lilting rhythm as if someone were speaking. The sentence fragment in the last five lines mimics the way one carries on casual conversation.)

Writing

QUICK ASSESS

Do students' responses:

✓ show understanding of the similarities and differences among sonnets, haiku, and free verse?

✓ explain why free verse is a form of poetry?

As they create a graphic to show the similarities and the differences among sonnets, haiku, and free verse, remind students to look at the categories of purpose, structure, rhyme, and rhythm. They may even want to create a three-circle Venn diagram to compare all three forms before explaining why free verse is considered a form of poetry.

READING AND WRITING EXTENSIONS

➤ Encourage students to look up some of Edgar Lee Masters's other works—essays, biographies, poems, plays, or fiction. Ask them to report orally on some of the major themes in the selections they read.

➤ Have students work with a partner to choose a poem written in free verse. Ask them to rewrite it in haiku verse.

See also Answer Key, page 123

Unit Overview

This unit is designed to help students understand the various techniques that persuasive writers use to convince an audience. As students analyze speeches by Abraham Lincoln, Martin Luther King, Jr., and Robert F. Kennedy, they will explore how writers state their views directly, create a convincing tone, choose effective words, and use personal experiences and brainstorming to make their arguments persuasive.

Literature Focus

	Lesson	Literature
1.	Viewpoint	**Abraham Lincoln,** "Gettysburg Address" (Nonfiction)
2.	Tone	**Martin Luther King, Jr.,** "I Have a Dream" (Nonfiction)
3.	Word Choice	
4.	Personal Experience	**Robert F. Kennedy,** "On the Death of Martin Luther King, Jr." (Nonfiction)
5.	Brainstorming	

Reading Focus

1. Persuasive writers often state their viewpoints directly. As a reader, you need to take time to reflect on the writer's viewpoint and decide if you agree with it.

2. An author's tone can often give clues about the author's message and his or her feelings about the subject.

3. Persuasive writers know that word choice contributes to the effectiveness of an argument.

4. Persuasive writers often use personal experiences as support for their arguments. Readers often find it easy to relate to these "real" stories.

5. When you read persuasive writing, look for the use of brainstorming. Persuasive writers often use this technique to help readers feel involved in the argument.

Writing Focus

1. Write a diary entry from two different points of view.
2. Compare and contrast the tone of two different speeches.
3. Rewrite a speech and compare its effectiveness to that of the original.
4. Write a memorandum offering advice on rewriting a speech.
5. Write a paragraph using brainstorming to persuade your audience to agree with your points.

One Viewpoint

C r i t i c a l   R e a d i n g

FOCUS

Viewpoints are often stated directly:

"…this nation, under God, shall have a new birth of freedom; and that government of the people, by the people, for the people, shall not perish from the earth."

BACKGROUND

In this lesson, students have an opportunity to read and respond to Abraham Lincoln's "Gettysburg Address." Over 48,000 lives were lost in the three days of fighting at Gettysburg, Pennsylvania. When President Lincoln was asked to speak at the dedication ceremony, he wanted to honor those who fell in battle and to speak to the future of our country. Using the *Bible* and works of Shakespeare as literary influences, Lincoln delivered a visionary speech so simple and eloquent that it is still remembered more than 130 years later.

➤ In his speech, Lincoln refers to three different images of America. One is from the past, as he describes a nation that was created "four score and seven years ago." The image of the present is at the ceremony itself, when Lincoln refers to dedicating the battlefield to those who gave their lives. Finally, Lincoln focuses on the future as he tries to persuade citizens to rededicate themselves to preserving democracy. His prose is powerfully persuasive when he asks Americans to "resolve that these dead shall not have died in vain," proclaims that the nation "shall have a new birth of freedom," and exhorts that our democracy "shall not perish from the earth." Students should have no trouble identifying Lincoln's viewpoint.

FOR DISCUSSION AND REFLECTION

➤ What images strike you as particularly effective? (Students may note Lincoln's depiction of the nation as something alive. He refers to the idea of life when he says our fathers "brought forth" and "a new birth of freedom.")

➤ What does Lincoln see as a huge challenge for the country? (In the second paragraph, he says the war is testing whether or not a nation founded on the ideals of liberty and equality can continue to exist.)

➤ What do you think Lincoln's purpose was in giving this speech? (Answers should include dedication of the cemetery, honoring the soldiers who died, remembering the reason for the battle, and persuading his audience to work hard to preserve democracy.)

W r i t i n g

QUICK ASSESS

Do students' diary entries:

✓ reflect Lincoln's viewpoint?

✓ reflect the viewpoint of a member of his audience?

As students write the diary entry that reflects Lincoln's viewpoint, encourage them to think of the huge responsibility and guilt he must have felt for the many lost lives. And as they write as a member of the audience, encourage them to imagine how they would feel as the mother or father of a son who has died here. Do they blame Lincoln? Are they bitter in their grief?

READING AND WRITING EXTENSIONS

➤ Bring in the editorial pages of several newspapers. Ask students to study one or two editorials and identify the writer's viewpoint in each.

➤ Invite students to work in small groups to research different aspects of the fighting at Gettysburg and Lincoln's role in the latter part of the war.

See also Answer Key, page 123

Two Tone

Critical Reading

FOCUS
An author's tone can help convince readers of his or her viewpoint:

"'Free at last! free at last! thank God Almighty, we are free at last!'"

BACKGROUND
On August 28, 1963, Martin Luther King, Jr., delivered his renowned "I Have a Dream" speech to an unprecedented gathering of 250,000 people at the Lincoln Memorial in Washington, D.C., a crowd there to rally for jobs and civil rights. In 1964, Dr. King was awarded the Nobel Peace Prize and later was the first African American honored by *Time* magazine as "Man of the Year."

➤ King's tone is serious and earnest in the beginning of his speech, but not so solemn as that of Lincoln in his "Gettysburg Address." Perhaps more than any other speaker, King set the tone in his speeches by using the technique of repetition. His words "grab" the crowd and move them toward his viewpoint through repetition of such phrases as "one hundred years later" and "now is the time" and "we can never be satisfied." He ends on a positive, almost joyful note when he repeats, "Free at last" like the ringing of a bell, again and again and again. The words were spoken with passion and stirred the crowd into a patriotic fervor. Try to bring in a recording of King's speech for the students to hear.

FOR DISCUSSION AND REFLECTION
➤ Where does the line "Let freedom ring" come from and what does it really mean? (The phrase is from the song, "My Country 'Tis of Thee," and it is used as a metaphor to symbolize patriotic feelings; freedom must prevail.)

➤ Does King think America is a great nation? (Students should see that King suggests that all people must be free of injustice and treated fairly and equally in order for America to be a great country.)

➤ What is King's definition of the American Dream? (It has nothing to do with money or possessions, but with races sitting down together, working together, praying together, and struggling together.)

Writing

QUICK ASSESS
Do students' responses:

✓ show understanding of tone and viewpoint?

✓ explain the similarities and differences between Lincoln's and King's tone?

✓ describe their feelings about each speech?

Make sure that as students note the differences in tone that they don't confuse tone with mood. *Tone* is the author's attitude toward a subject, while *mood* means the atmosphere or feeling within the work. For instance, Lincoln's tone is serious, but the mood is somber and hushed.

READING AND WRITING EXTENSIONS
➤ Invite students to write an original speech or poem using this sentence from the speech as their opening sentence: "I have a dream today."

➤ Encourage students to work together in the spirit of Martin Luther King to create a mural that depicts a visual representation of his dream. This could be displayed on a bulletin board or painted permanently on an appropriate wall.

Three Word Choice

Critical Reading

FOCUS

Persuasive language includes carefully chosen words that appeal to the mind and the heart:

"Continue to work with the faith that unearned suffering is redemptive."

BACKGROUND

To convince the reader to think and act a certain way, writers must choose their words very carefully. Their viewpoints need to appeal to both the mind and the emotions of their audiences—whether in newspaper editorials, speeches, advertisements, essays, or in commercials.

➤ In Lesson Three, students have the opportunity to review King's and Lincoln's speeches in detail, picking out words that set the tone of the piece and, at the same time, help to convince the reader. The unique words in King's speech gain the reader's attention easily. Since King was a Baptist minister, he was used to building momentum toward an emotionally charged conclusion. "Quest for freedom," "trials and tribulations," "storms of persecution," and "veterans of creative suffering" are all phrases that suggest passion and emotion.

FOR DISCUSSION AND REFLECTION

➤ Why does King repeat *you* so often in his speech? (Students may note that it's as if he is speaking to each individual directly.)

➤ What images do you find especially striking? (Some students may point to the description that people have been "battered by the storms of persecution and staggered by the winds of police brutality." King is comparing the inequality of segregation and the violence displayed by authority toward blacks to the ravaged destruction caused by storms and winds.)

➤ Based on the viewpoint in his speech, how do you think King felt about the Vietnam War? (Ask students to explain their reasoning as they offer answers. As a peace-loving man, King abhorred America's involvement in Vietnam and spoke out against it.)

Writing

QUICK ASSESS

Do students' responses:

✓ reflect the "feel" of King's speech?

✓ explain the effectiveness of their rewriting?

As they try to rewrite Dr. King's speech, students should soon realize that without using his powerful techniques of repetition, imagery, and careful word choice, much of the strength of the speech will be lost. Have students read their revisions aloud to a partner and then discuss how their writing could be made more dramatic and persuasive.

READING AND WRITING EXTENSIONS

➤ Encourage students to listen to the news on the TV or radio, paying special attention to the word choice of any speeches they hear. Ask them to write a paragraph evaluating the effectiveness of one that used distinctive language.

➤ Invite students to reread Lincoln's "Gettysburg Address." Have them make a list of all of the words and phrases that they find especially effective and then compare their lists to those of their classmates.

Four Personal Experience

Critical Reading

Focus

Personal experiences can provide convincing support in persuasive writing:

"I had a member of my family killed, but he was killed by a white man."

Background

Robert F. Kennedy (1925–1968) was, like Martin Luther King, Jr., a powerful civil rights leader. He believed that individual action could overcome injustice and oppression, similar to Dr. King's ideas. Kennedy's powerful oratory continues to inspire generations to change the world, three decades following his own assassination in 1968, at the age of 43. The Robert F. Kennedy Memorial has been dedicated to perpetuating his vision by encouraging respect for human rights and justice in the United States and around the world.

➤ Students should quickly see the similarity in oratory style between King and Kennedy. They both choose words carefully and use repetition to strengthen their points. The speeches are both powerful and emotional and use historical allusions as support—King citing the Book of Isaiah in the *Bible* and Kennedy mentioning the Greek poets. Kennedy's use of personal experience in reference to the assassination of J.F.K. makes his speech even more poignant; the reader easily makes a personal connection to the death of a loved one.

For Discussion and Reflection

➤ What is the main idea of Robert Kennedy's speech? (Answers should include that Kennedy wants all people to rise above hatred and violence, to learn to live together.)

➤ Why does Kennedy use repetition in his speech? (He wants to emphasize different ideas and obtain the reader's attention.)

➤ How effective is the ending of his speech? (Responses will vary. Some students may notice that his use of *dedicate* gives a "Lincoln" feel to his closing.)

Writing

Quick Assess

Do students' memos:

✓ reflect understanding of what makes a powerful speech?

✓ show how personal experiences support an argument?

✓ evaluate the effectiveness of Kennedy's argument?

Students will likely agree that this is a powerful speech, especially if they hear it spoken aloud. Encourage students to discuss its effectiveness before they write their memos. Students may decide, for example, in their memos that Kennedy's speech is powerful but could have used more support for the argument or a different closing.

Reading and Writing Extensions

➤ Invite students to consider Robert F. Kennedy's statement, "Some men see things as they are and say why. I dream things that never were and say why not." Ask them to write about what they think Kennedy meant and whether they think his sentence describes themselves.

➤ Have students create a drawing, painting, or collage that depicts the main idea of this phrase from Kennedy's speech, ". . . to tame the savageness of man and to make gentle the life of this world."

See also Answer Key, page 123

Five Brainstorming

Critical Reading

FOCUS

Brainstorming is a powerful persuasive technique that makes the reader feel involved:

"…it is perhaps well to ask what kind of a nation we are and what direction we want to move in."

BACKGROUND

Students may be familiar with brainstorming as a process of generating new ideas. The persuasive technique of brainstorming may be new to them. The spirited, give-and-take banter of creative brainstorming is what persuasive writers are trying to get down on paper, to draw in and persuade their audience. This "thinking aloud" technique allows the writer to voice both the pros and cons of an argument, allowing readers to follow along in the thought process as if they were having an intimate conversation with the writer. In other words, the writer is talking "with" readers, not "at" them. Students should agree that it's easier to connect to a topic when they feel personally involved.

➤ Lesson Five illustrates the brainstorming technique in Robert Kennedy's "On the Death of Martin Luther King, Jr." speech. He asks questions and answers them with negative choices and positive choices. The listener then contemplates different options as Kennedy points out the consequences of several plans of action. Through this technique, Kennedy not only involves his audience emotionally but intellectually. Kennedy's audience feels interested and involved as they ponder the possible courses of action.

FOR DISCUSSION AND REFLECTION

➤ What behavior does Kennedy oppose and what does he support? (Kennedy does not want Americans to feel bitterness, revenge, and hatred. Those emotions would polarize the nation. Instead, Kennedy wants Americans to make an effort to understand with compassion and love to avoid "the stain of bloodshed.")

➤ What do you think people would think of this speech in the '90s? (Answers will vary.)

➤ Have you ever used the technique of brainstorming in an argument? (Encourage students to describe situations that come to mind.)

Writing

QUICK ASSESS

Do students' paragraphs:

✓ include one or two points from their notes?

✓ use brainstorming as a persuasive technique?

Students should have no problem relating to the technique of brainstorming because it is so often used to introduce classroom discussions. You might suggest that students think of "pros" and "cons" as points to include in developing their own personal topics.

READING AND WRITING EXTENSIONS

➤ Encourage students to complete their outline and write their persuasive speech. After they present their speeches to the class, discuss how effective the brainstorming techniques were.

➤ Challenge students to write a paragraph comparing Kennedy's statements to the Golden Rule: "Do unto others as you would have them do unto you." How similar are they?

See also Answer Key, page 124

U n i t   O v e r v i e w

In this unit, students will explore the writings of Mark Twain. As they read and respond to excerpts from a short story, two novels, his autobiography, and two personal letters, students will have the opportunity to observe how Mark Twain commented on human nature and society by using humor and satire.

L i t e r a t u r e   F o c u s

	Lesson	Literature
1.	Early Attempts at Humor	from "My First Literary Venture" (Short Story)
2.	Exaggeration	from *Life on the Mississippi* (Autobiography)
3.	The Art of Satire	from *A Connecticut Yankee in King Arthur's Court* (Fiction)
4.	Humor in Character	from *The Adventures of Huckleberry Finn* (Fiction)
5.	A Man of Letters	from personal letters (Letters)

R e a d i n g   F o c u s

1. Writers have many reasons for using humor. Although humor can be used to make a point, writers sometimes use humor simply to entertain.

2. Authors use exaggeration not only to entertain and add humor, but also to give insights into characters.

3. When you come across satire in your reading, keep in mind that its purpose is to ridicule or convey amusement to make a point or affect change.

4. Writers can use humor to reveal what characters are like.

5. Personal letters can provide insights into a writer, both through their subject matter and their tone.

W r i t i n g   F o c u s

1. List reasons that writers use humor.

2. Analyze Twain's use of exaggeration to create humor in a story.

3. Examine examples of satire.

4. Explain how humor affects the perception of a character.

5. Explain whether or not Twain uses humor to teach his readers.

One Early Attempts at Humor

Critical Reading

FOCUS

One reason authors use humor is to entertain:

"I thought it was desperately funny, and was densely unconscious that there was any moral obliquity about such a publication."

BACKGROUND

Lesson One is an introduction to the humor of Mark Twain. Students should be able to see the twinkle in Twain's eye and the start of a smile on his face as he made up his mind to edit one issue of his uncle's newspaper, the *Weekly Hannibal Journal*. It's obvious that even as a thirteen-year-old, Twain had the intelligence and wit to pull off a good joke. And, as he reflected on the incident many years later, it's easy to see how Twain felt comfortable, both as a younster and as an adult, using his subtle, yet keen, sense of humor to entertain others.

FOR DISCUSSION AND REFLECTION

➤ What are some examples of humor in this selection? (Responses may include that Twain would publicly make fun of people's problems, that he would go to so much trouble to even make a picture, that he ended up being friends with the editor, and that he got two years of turnips.)

➤ How does Twain's word choice add to the humor? (Students' answers will vary. Twain uses formal phrases like "elaborately wretched account," "gratuitous rascality," and "escaped dissection" to amuse readers.)

➤ Do you notice any irony that also lends humor? (Help students to see that instead of getting in serious trouble at the paper—as one would imagine—Twain actually helps the circulation of the paper increase by thirty-three subscribers.)

Writing

QUICK ASSESS

Do students' responses:

✓ list several reasons why authors use humor in their writing?

✓ circle ones that apply to Twain's writing?

As background for reading this selection, discuss with students some of their ideas about the careers they want to pursue. Ask how many of them think they know now at age thirteen exactly what career they want to have. Some of the reasons that writers use humor might include to emphasize a point, soften a serious message, create a dramatic effect, or just plain have fun.

READING AND WRITING EXTENSIONS

➤ Invite students to write a humorous newspaper article about an incident from their childhood where they've poked fun at themselves or someone else.

➤ Encourage students to write about an event that didn't seem very funny at the time, but later on seemed hilarious—perhaps when they were the brunt of a joke or the central focus of an awkward situation. Then have students share their writings with the class.

See also Answer Key, page 124

Two Exaggeration

Critical Reading

FOCUS

Exaggeration, or hyperbole, is a form of humor favored by Mark Twain:

"You dredge an alligator once and he's *convinced*. It's the last you hear of *him*. He wouldn't come back for pie."

BACKGROUND

Students can have fun with Mark Twain's humor in Lesson Two, as they see him banter back and forth with the riverboat pilot whom he had known twenty-five years earlier. Again, be sure that students understand Twain's situational irony, how he develops the humor because the pilot is oblivious to the fact that Twain knows his story is pure fabrication. Help students find specific examples of Twain's exaggeration, such as the need to dredge out alligators because they were so thick, the difficulties of piloting because of alligators, and the natural talent for judging and smelling alligator waters. Students should smile, with Twain, that when alligators see a boat coming "they break camp and go for the woods."

➤ Mark Twain provides an excellent example of an author who wrote about what he knew and who he was. Born Samuel Langhorne Clemens, he took his pen name from the phrase used by boatmen taking depth measures, by calling out *mark* (by their measure), *twain* (two) fathoms deep, which was a safe depth. His adventuresome growing-up years in Hannibal, Missouri, and his experiences on the Mississippi River as a steamboat apprentice and pilot combined to provide rich background material for his works.

FOR DISCUSSION AND REFLECTION

➤ Why does Twain describe Rob Styles as a "slim enough cub, in my time"? (Twenty-five years before, Rob Styles was a beginner or apprentice riverboat pilot, the person who steers the ship.)

➤ What does the phrase "as a burglar knows a roundsman" mean? (A burglar is aware of a guard's schedule as he makes "rounds" or inspects a building or property.)

➤ Predict how you think the story will end. (Ask students to refer to specific text details as they explain their predictions.)

Writing

QUICK ASSESS
Do students' responses:

✓ show understanding of Twain's exaggeration?

✓ comment on their opinion of the pilot?

As they write about Twain's exaggeration, help students to see that the sarcastic thoughts that Twain kept to himself are indications of his feelings for the pilot.

READING AND WRITING EXTENSIONS

➤ Invite students to write a paragraph describing a particular skill or talent they have—for example, playing basketball, singing, skiing, or remembering names and faces. Have them greatly exaggerate their abilities to produce a humorous piece.

➤ Look together at selected Currier and Ives prints that were popular and affordable in Twain's lifetime. Ask students to write about why they do or do not like a particular one.

See also Answer Key, page 124

Three The Art of Satire

C r i t i c a l R e a d i n g

FOCUS

Mark Twain uses satire to poke fun in a lighthearted manner: Armor is "very heavy and is nearly the uncomfortablest material in the world for a nightshirt, yet plenty used it for that—tax-collectors, and reformers, and one-horse kings with a defective title, and those sorts of people ...."

BACKGROUND

Students may find it more difficult to recognize Mark Twain's use of satire than they did his use of exaggeration. They may need several readings of the excerpt in Lesson Three before they realize that it is even funny, for Twain's humor is subtle. In his frontier style of journalism, Twain showed an American disfavor of pomp and circumstance, stuffiness, and tradition. His gentle ribbing in *A Connecticut Yankee in King Arthur's Court* is meant to make a point, not enemies. And once again, as in many of his works, we see youth as the star of the story.

➤ If possible, bring in Hal Holbrook's recording *Mark Twain Tonight*, from his one-man show about Mark Twain, for students to enjoy.

FOR DISCUSSION AND REFLECTION

➤ Point out some examples of satire in the selection. (Responses might include the exaggeration in the armor's description, the process of being carried and helped to get on the horse, and the ridiculousness of his ride out of town.)

➤ What is Twain really satirizing in this story? (Students need to understand that Twain is bringing to light his feelings about how ridiculous the English customs of knights and armor and duels seem to people in nineteenth-century Connecticut.)

➤ What does Twain think about boys? (They are mischievous, but refreshingly honest and unassuming: "In my experience boys are the same in all ages.")

W r i t i n g

QUICK ASSESS

Do students' responses:

✓ list several humorous examples?

✓ show understanding of satire and how it is used to create humor?

Before beginning this lesson you might recall with students the fairy tale "The Emperor's New Clothes" and its theme about vanity. Have students read this excerpt from *A Connecticut Yankee in King Arthur's Court*, silently first and then aloud so that students understand the language and get the full effect of Twain's spoof. Satire is a type of humor that some students may not be used to, so lots of discussion will help them think about what is funny and why.

READING AND WRITING EXTENSIONS

➤ Encourage students to find contemporary examples of satire to share with the class. Suggest that they search newspaper editorials, political cartoons, comic strips, advertisements, or comedy monologues for examples.

➤ Have students design a caricature of the "Connecticut Yankee" based on Twain's description of the armor and shield.

See also Answer Key, page 124

Four Humor in Character

Critical Reading

FOCUS

FOCUS

Authors use humor to give the reader insight into a character: "Then she told me all about the bad place, and I said I wished I was there. She got mad, then, but I didn't mean no harm. All I wanted was to go somewheres; all I wanted was a change, I warn't particular."

BACKGROUND

Mark Twain captures the heart of youth in his stories. His writing seems to stem from a combination of experience and a great imagination; he describes the best adventures that kids could ever have or wish to have. Most every young person has longed to run away and be free of responsibility and authority. The reader can't help but be right there with Huck and Tom, peeking over their shoulders, urging them on, every step of the way.

➤ In Lesson Four, Twain's description of Huckleberry Finn shows how his droll humor can depict a character and also displays Twain's expertise with dialect. Students should understand that dialect, as a form of language, is representative of different regions of the country. It's influenced by pronunciation, grammar, and word choice, and using it is a natural way to bring characters to life. For instance, from the very first sentence—with its colloquialisms and the use of *ain't*—one knows that Huck is probably from somewhere in the country and not interested in education. The reader immediately makes a mental picture and maybe even a mental judgment.

FOR DISCUSSION AND REFLECTION

➤ Give some examples of dialect that offer insight about Huckleberry. (Answers might include "with some stretchers," "fetched us a dollar a day apiece," "grumble a little over the victuals," "she worked me middling hard," and she "learned me about Moses.")

➤ How does Huck feel about Bible stories? (He's not interested in hearing about dead people.)

➤ Does Huck seem honest? (Students may think probably yes. Huck says exactly what he thinks and voices his opinion without worrying about the consequences, such as noticing Widow Douglas's snuff habit when she said she was against smoking or saying that he wished he was in the "bad place" rather than being where he was.)

Writing

QUICK ASSESS

Do students' explanations:

✓ show understanding of Twain's humor?

✓ explain their perception of Huck Finn's character?

As students start to write about the character of Huck, help them to see that he is not just a humorous backwoods youngster. Suggest that they try to appreciate what he represents. As they think of him in a more serious light, students might see him as an outcast and a loner, one who defies authority and is constantly in trouble, one who will never make it in the real world. Without Twain's humor, Huck really wouldn't be very likable, and he might seem more like an ignorant rebel.

READING AND WRITING EXTENSIONS

➤ Ask students to draw a sketch of what they think Huckleberry Finn looks like based on their reading of the passage in Lesson Four.

➤ Invite students to read and act out in class Mark Twain's hilarious tale, "The Celebrated Jumping Frog of Calaveras County."

Five A Man of Letters

Critical Reading

FOCUS

Letters give us insight into their author:

"They have expelled Huck from their library as 'trash and suitable only for the slums.' That will sell 25,000 copies for us sure."

BACKGROUND

At one point in Twain's life, between 1862 and 1865, he was prospecting for gold in Nevada and California. But after the mines failed, he went broke. He then supported himself with his writing career and gave up his "golden dreams" for good. He fell in love with a picture of Olivia Langdon and became determined to marry her. Because his lecture schedule kept him so busy, he had to correspond with her by writing more than one hundred love letters. Finally, in 1870, Olivia Langdon consented to become his wife. Students may find it difficult to think of the humorous Twain writing a love letter, but remind them that during this time period everyone wrote letters.

➤ Explain that in Twain's era, people took pride in their handwriting and spent a portion of their day keeping up with their correspondence. Today, people are used to telephone answering machines and E-Mail and seldom sit down to write something out with pen and ink. But for many, nothing can take the place of a beautifully written note that seems personal and genuine.

FOR DISCUSSION AND REFLECTION

➤ Why do you think people disapproved of *The Adventures of Huckleberry Finn*? (Students may point to the description of Jim, the slave, or to the sometimes bawdy humor.)

➤ Why would a book sell more if it had been labeled as "trash"? (Negative publicity may arouse people's curiosity; they'll want to see what all of the fuss is about.)

➤ Why is the second letter an interesting contrast to the first? (Students may point out that it reveals to us not a crisp wit but an affectionate and sensitive side of Mark Twain that isn't always noticeable in his writing.)

Writing

QUICK ASSESS

Do students' analyses:

✔ focus on one of Twain's writings?

✔ explain whether Twain's writing uses humor without "preaching"?

Students should enjoy examining the letters that show the human side of Mark Twain. Class discussion will help them understand how the various selections in the unit reveal different dimensions of Mark Twain, the man. This discussion should help students choose their favorite piece and write about how it does or does not use humor to teach something to readers without "preaching."

READING AND WRITING EXTENSIONS

➤ Have students write a humorous character sketch, using regional dialect, about a favorite friend, a relative, or a book or television show character.

➤ Encourage students to write a sincere letter of appreciation to some influential person in their life, expressing thanks for what the person has meant to them. Invite students to consider mailing their final drafts to the person as a surprise.

See also Answer Key, page 124

Most activities in the *Daybook* ask for open-ended, creative responses. As a result, only selected activities for which specific answers are possible are included here. The intent is to help you, the teacher, by clarifying a possible or partial response to the question, not to specify the one complete, true answer. Answers are given here only for teachers who want further clarification of specific activities.

PAGE 12: Students' ideas about the theme of the poem will vary. One statement of a theme might be this: The narrator thinks that no matter in what ways he and the instructor are alike, they are still different, and whatever the narrator writes for English B, it will be viewed through the eyes of a white person. Thus, his theme may be judged in a different light than that of a white student.

PAGE 16: Students' charts will differ. Following is one sample:

	"The Weary Blues"	"Theme for English B"
What is the effect of Hughes's choice of words in the poem?	has a rhythm, is like listening to music	makes me thoughtful about the differences between people
Does Hughes use figurative language (such as similes and metaphors)? What does it add to the poem?	"He slept like a rock or a man that's dead." emphasizes "weary"; paints a distinct picture of that "weary" man sleeping	no
What is the style of the poem (for example, is it conversational)? How does the style affect you as you read?	informal, like storytelling, makes me want to read or listen to find out what happens next	conversational, involves me as if I were talking or listening to Hughes
How do sound devices reflect the meaning of the poem?	arrangement of lines (repeated, like a song's chorus) emphasizes the comparison of the poem to blues music and the "blue" (sad) nature of the singer's tale	not important

PAGE 19: Students' answers will vary, but should include that Hughes knew of the rich cultural and historical heritage of African Americans and that he thought many people were not aware of this heritage.

PAGE 21: Students' timelines will differ. Here is a sample:

1902		1929		1940s	1967
Birth	grew up in Cleveland, Kansas City, and Chicago ("Aunt Sue's Stories")	graduated from college, lived in New Jersey ("Theme for English B")	in Haiti, thinking about his writing	Wrote for *Chicago Defender* ("The Return of Simple")	Death

PAGE 31: Here is a sample web and paragraph:

"great day"

"proud graduating class of 1940"

"thanked God … He had allowed me to see this day"

graduation =
pride, reward for hard work, chance to stand in spotlight

watch was the "dream of a day"

"my hard-earned diploma"

looked "like a sunbeam" in dress

The narrator in "I Know Why the Caged Bird Sings" obviously worked hard in school and looked forward with great pride to graduation day. She anticipated the honors and praise she would receive for her hard work. Instead, her day was almost ruined by administrators who talked to her graduating class about a nearby school of white students who would receive new science equipment and programs, while they praised black students for their athletic ability. This made the narrator feel angry and sad at the same time, because she wanted to be appreciated for her intelligence and hard work, just as white people were. She felt proud again when a fellow student stood and began singing the "Negro national anthem."

PAGE 34: Students' answers will differ, but they should mention that Myers is writing about how important the *Brown vs. Board of Education of Topeka* decision was to ending legal segregation in the United States. Details in the text that point to this idea include:

- In the case, it was known that "If segregation in the schools was declared unconstitutional, then *all* segregation in public places could be declared unconstitutional."
- It was argued that segregation made African American children feel inferior.
- It was argued that segregation made President Eisenhower's administration look bad to other governments.
- It was argued that segregation deprived African Americans of equal opportunity.
- "The high court's decision in *Brown vs. Board of Education* signaled an important change in the struggle for civil rights."

Students will choose different graphic organizers to use in displaying their arguments. One example would be a web with the theme in the middle and each of the above points radiating out on the arms.

PAGE 42: Students will choose to list different images. One list might look like this:

Images of sight	Images of touch
Tall range of mountains with "sheltering shadows"	White powdery dust in a "smothering blanket"
Squat tar-papered barracks sitting in a pool of white dust	Road is "soft with churned up dust"
Boy Scouts looked like "flour-dusted cookies"	Sank into road's dust as if "plowing through a snow bank"
Dreary place, no trees or grass, "sun-bleached desert"	Dust "sifting" into eyes, nose, and mouth

Students may write of different moods. One example would be a "dreary" mood brought on by reading about such a stark, bleak place where one can't breathe freely or see anything colorful.

PAGE 45: Students will list various qualities for Kit. One list might look like this:

What Kit Is Like	How I Know
Impulsive	Author tells us in second line of excerpt; again when she tells the captain to turn back for the doll; and when she jumps into the water
Has a temper	Is angry at captain for ignoring her
Athletic	Swims well

PAGE 51:
The plot of this excerpt is not shaped as a climb up and down a mountain, but rather a walk up one side of a mountain to the top (exposition, rising action, climax), where it stops. The falling action and resolution are left to the reader's imagination. Students will choose different graphic organizers to describe this plot line. A timeline might look like this:

Climax
Melinda Alice rushing to her seat in class, mind racing about being late and not studying for her test, idly wishing she were dead

Rising Action
Melinda Alice finding a snail, who grants three wishes, and wishing for a thousand wishes

Exposition
Description of Melinda Alice

PAGE 53:
Among possible themes or lessons about which students may write are the following: "Be careful what you wish for; you may get it," or "Evil is punished."

PAGE 57:
Students should have placed an X next to Brooks's theme, which she states in the last paragraph: "The truth was, if you got a good Tragedy out of a lifetime, one good, ripping tragedy, thorough, unridiculous, bottom-scraping, *not* the issue of human stupidity, you were doing, she thought, very well, you were doing well."

Students' opinions about what Brooks is trying to say will differ. One example might look like this:

Brooks is trying to say that we all have tragedy in our lives, but we have to make the best of it by finding something to laugh at or something to be happy about.

Students will cite different details from the story to support their version of the theme. The example of the "blooms" is discussed on this page. Students may write that Brooks thinks that the middle-aged men in the story are tragic because these men don't have anything better to do than stand on a street corner. Maud Martha thinks that life can be tragic, but she can always find something to laugh at in the midst of tragedy, the silver lining in any cloud. She also thinks that many people experience so much tragedy in their lives that if you have only one tragedy happen for which you're not responsible, you have a nice life.

PAGE 59:
Students' interpretations of the meaning of the elephant will vary. For example, students might write that the poet is comparing herself to a strong animal who is caged. The elephant enjoys performing for zoo visitors but hates the quiet of the night. Similarly, perhaps the poet enjoys having an audience and is sad and lonely when she doesn't have it.

Students' answers in the chart will also differ. Here is a sample:

What does this poem tell you about ...

the speaker's feelings about herself?	the difference between how things "look" and what they actually are like?
The speaker sounds lonely, as if she wants the company of others. She likes praise from others but is sad when she doesn't have it.	The poem substitutes the whole image of the elephant in the zoo for a person "caged" in by loneliness. Something or someone that looks powerful can feel lonely.

PAGE 62: Students' ideas about the theme of the fable will differ. Some may believe the theme involves materialism. Another example might look like this:

People don't suddenly change their character; people who have acted in a greedy, selfish fashion all their lives will most likely continue to be greedy and selfish.

Students will probably not all choose the same suitor for the princess, and their endings will surprise you. For example, if a student has the princess choose the poor suitor, the theme might change to: "A greedy, selfish person can change if he or she meets the right person."

PAGE 66: Possible themes include:

• A parent's love shines through when he or she cares for a sick child.

• Poor communication can sometimes lead to misunderstandings.

• Ignorance is not always bliss and can cause undue worry.

• In the absence of information, people will often substitute hearsay for truth.

The primary theme is the last one, because it is supported by and explains the events of the story. The boy spends the entire story looking wan and pale despite the fact that all evidence pointed to a quick recovery:

• His fever was 102°, which is not dangerous in children, as we find out from the father.

• The doctor determines that the boy has a light case of the flu, "and there was no danger if you avoided pneumonia."

• He is given his medication on time.

• His father enjoys a hunting trip that afternoon, confident that the boy is not too sick to be left.

No one in the story communicates to the boy that he is not dangerously ill. In his ignorance of both his condition and of the difference between the two temperature scales, he bases his unfounded fear of dying on things he has heard from other boys.

PAGE 67: Students' answers will vary but should be substantiated with citations from the story. For example:

1. Parents misunderstand their children.   Disagree (not a possible theme)

Papa didn't misunderstand Schatz, because Schatz never told him anything that could be misunderstood. He never told him anything at all, other than short answers about how sick he felt. There is no proof for this theme.

PAGE 73: Heaney is comparing constructing a building to building a relationship between two people. They are similar in that both need a solid foundation on which to build, and both involve connecting two things (bricks, people). Students will probably find other similarities.

PAGE 74: Students will interpret these lines differently. One interpretation is that when relationships age, the connections between two people may begin to erode, but the foundation is still there. A less optimistic interpretation might be that the two people in the poem's relationship have built a wall between them, so they no longer need to make any pretense about trying to be connected to each other.

PAGE 76: A sample Venn diagram might look like this:

assonance   both   consonance

fire ice I've desire I twice suffice   suffice ice twice   some say twice suffice tasted ice

Students will offer different opinions on what sound devices add to the poem. One point is that the word choice, the emphasis, and the repeated use of the sounds of "fire" and "ice" add to the alternative warm and cold feelings throughout the poem.

PAGE 81: Students' descriptions of Saroyan's physical setting and mood will vary but may mention the following points:

- At home in a Paris neighborhood
- "A very hot afternoon in August"
- Sitting at a card table
- Father and daughter dressed casually and barefoot
- "both of them just being there, and not being excited or anything"

PAGE 82: Words that describe the mood are *casual*, *calm*, *friendly*, *relaxed*, *homey*. Saroyan uses details, such as the descriptions of the characters' clothing and mention of the fact that they're barefoot, to let the reader know that the atmosphere is comfortable and relaxed. These details tell the reader even more about the mood than do his descriptions of the physical setting.

PAGE 86: Students will write differing opinions about this statement. For example, a student who disagrees with the statement might write:

Gaston does not symbolize the father's loneliness in the story. Instead, Gaston and his sudden appearance symbolize the father, who is seeing his daughter for the first time in a long time and who finds out that they are very different people. The daughter lives with her mother in New York, while the father later compares his cozy home to Gaston's home in the peach seed.

The father does not fit into his daughter's life in New York and it's obvious that he and the mother are also very different. In her phone call to the daughter, the mother indicates that she thinks the father is odd, different from other people, with different ideas. Similarly, Saroyan writes that Gaston "wandered around the plate, but everything seemed wrong and he didn't know what to do or where to go," because he didn't fit there. His home is in the peach pit. At the end of the story, after the daughter goes home with the mother, the father says he feels a bit like Gaston on the plate, out of place in his daughter's life.

PAGE 90: Students' expressions of the thesis statement will differ. One example might look like this:

Many people have written untrue or inaccurate stories about Native Americans, and these have been taught to American schoolchildren as truth.

Students' opinions of the thesis will also vary.

PAGE 91: Following is the beginning of a sample chart:

Reasons	Evidence
Indians are inaccurately portrayed as killers.	Indian victories are called "massacres"; white victories are called "battles."
Indians are inaccurately portrayed as treacherous.	No mention is made of white men's treachery in breaking treaties with Indians.
Indians are murderers.	Indians killed in self-defense and to protect land are called "murderers"; white men who do the same are "patriots."

PAGES 96–97:   Students should have marked some of the following parts of the essay as fact:

- The first paragraph, in which Rooney describes his habit of throwing things away
- "Sometime around the year 500 B.C., the Greeks in Athens passed a law prohibiting people from throwing their garbage in the street."
- Chemical companies dumping their waste in rivers or stored them in drums
- Rooney storing chemicals in his garage
- "The people of the city of New York throw away nine times their weight in garbage and junk every year."
- "Of all household waste, 30 percent of the weight and 50 percent of the volume is the packaging that stuff comes in."
- "Americans spend more for the packaging of food than all of our farmers together make in income growing it."

PAGE 98:   Opinions will differ on the seriousness of the problems described in Rooney's essay. Students' charts will also differ, but most will show that facts can be checked at the library in books and encyclopedias as well as on the Internet.

PAGE 100:   Students' charts and supporting evidence will vary. Following is a sample chart:

Appeals to reason:	"Memorial and Recommendations …"	"Silencing the Sound of Music"	"America the Not-so-Beautiful"
statistics			X
examples	X	X	X
facts		X	X
Appeals to feelings:			
emotional language	X	X	X
humor		X	X
mention of basic values	X	X	X

PAGE 105:   Students will list different things on their charts. Here are a few examples of Summer's feelings:

- May and Ob: She's a big woman and he's artistic; both are old. They are making plans to make Summer's life there more pleasant: adding a swing and a tree house. Summer likes them and feels like living with them will be paradise.
- Shelves of whirligigs: She is impressed by the number of different types and finds them to be artistic.
- Thunderstorm whirligig: She likes it and is frightened by it.

PAGE 106:   Students' paragraphs will vary, but many may say that Summer values the simplicity of May and Ob and of their surroundings. She is impressed at their generosity at taking her in. Students might then write that Rylant has a respect and liking for simple, generous people, no matter what their home and other surroundings look like; there is more to a person than where he or she lives.

PAGE 108: Students' charts will vary. Following is a sample:

Elements of Rylant's Style	Examples from *Missing May*
Colorful, informal words	cockeyed, thunk, whirling
Informal speech patterns	"Uncle Ob will go down to Ellet's Grocery and get you."; "honey"
Long similes	Summer was treated "like a homework assignment somebody was always having to do"; compares herself to mice, "caged and begging"
Descriptive details	description of trailer; description of food in cabinets

PAGE 110: A sample of the speaker's thoughts might include that he's intimidated by Sandy Jane; he feels shy and awkward around her; he's nervous about talking to her; he doesn't like how he feels about himself when she leaves; he thinks he has something to do with her being popular; he hopes she likes him.

PAGE 111: Students' opinions about the boy being a "jerk" will vary. Their paragraphs about Rylant's perspective should include that the boy is introspective. He recognizes that he feels one way while acting another, but he doesn't understand himself enough to know why he acts as he does. Thus, he is an "outsider looking in."

PAGE 113: Rylant felt like an outsider because:

• Her home wasn't as new or as nice (in her view) as that of her friend.

• She was ashamed of her house and her neighborhood.

• She didn't think she was like "city kids," so she didn't go to the city library.

• She didn't like to leave her own town because other places made her feel not as good; they made her feel "dull and ugly and poor."

Students' writing about Rylant's perspective will vary but should include that she writes about outsiders because when she was younger, she had experiences that made her feel that way. Writers often pull from their own experiences to write.

PAGE 119: Students will express the facts about Eleanor Roosevelt differently. Here are examples:

Who is she? an older wife and mother

What is she describing? the process she went through when she "grew up" and became her own person

When is she writing? after this process has taken place, probably when she's older

How did she change? overcame her fears of other people, her need for approval and love from other people; learned to accept herself as she was and not care so much what other people thought of her

PAGE 120: Students' profiles will differ based on the facts they wrote.

PAGE 122: Students will interpret the poem differently. Below is one sample chart that shows the meanings of various lines in the poem. Student questions will vary considerably.

Lines from the poem	My paraphrase of what the poet is saying	Questions, comments, ideas
Because I could not stop for Death—	The speaker had not prepared for death.	What's with the unusual capitalization and punctuation?
He kindly stopped for me—	Death doesn't wait till you're prepared; it comes in its own time.	How can Death be kind?
The Carriage held but just Ourselves—	Everyone dies alone.	Is the speaker lonely?
The Dews drew quivering and chill—	All life "quivers" about facing death.	What time did the speaker die?
Since then—'tis Centuries—and yet	The speaker has been dead for hundreds of years and remembers it still.	When did the speaker live—and where?

PAGE 125: Following are some sample points that would support this interpretation of Dickinson's poem:

- The rhythm of the poem is slow and lyrical, not jarring, as if Death bounced into the narrator's life suddenly and violently.

- Many of the words Dickinson chooses all speak of a slow pace: "slowly," "no haste," "paused".

- Death is portrayed as courteous and kind, not rude and abrupt ("He kindly stopped," "His Civility").

- The images in the poem are relaxing and comforting: riding in a carriage (not a car or something faster), seeing children at recess (not hard at work), passing fields of grain, watching the setting sun.

PAGE 135:

Weekly Budget 1940

Income (approximate):	$50.00
Expenses:	
haircut	.50
doctor appointment	2.00
groceries:	
1 gal. milk	.52
1 doz. eggs	.35
2 loaves bread	.16
1 pound butter	.35
1 pound pork chops	.33
2 pounds chuck roast	.58
dinner out (for two)	3.25
new shirt	2.00
Total expenses:	$ 10.04

PAGE 136: Students' paragraphs will vary but will probably include such points as the following:

- There was no war in 1940; in 1942 the U. S. was involved in a war.

- Food items were plentiful in 1940; after 1942, many items were scarce because of the war.

- There was no rationing in 1940; after 1942 items were rationed.

- In 1940 you could buy a "good suit" or a "dressy wool dress." In 1942 many items of new clothing were made in a shoddy way.

- Not many families bought appliances in 1940 because they were luxuries; in 1942 not many bought them, and they were probably still luxuries, but they were also scarce and badly made.

PAGE 137: Students' wording will vary but should center around Phillips's main idea, which is that life in 1940 was simple. People didn't make a lot of money, but necessities didn't cost very much either.

PAGE 139: One reason Mr. Tanimoto survived was that he was two miles from the explosion. He protected himself by jumping between two big rocks in the garden and bellied up hard against one of the rocks trying to protect himself.

PAGE 140: A sample graphic below:

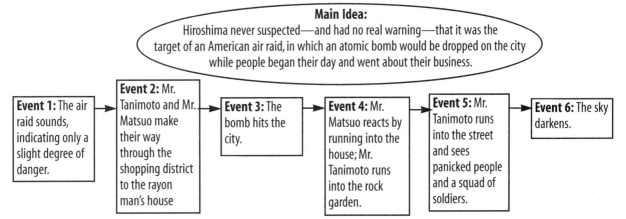

Main Idea:
Hiroshima never suspected—and had no real warning—that it was the target of an American air raid, in which an atomic bomb would be dropped on the city while people began their day and went about their business.

Event 1: The air raid sounds, indicating only a slight degree of danger.

Event 2: Mr. Tanimoto and Mr. Matsuo make their way through the shopping district to the rayon man's house

Event 3: The bomb hits the city.

Event 4: Mr. Matsuo reacts by running into the house; Mr. Tanimoto runs into the rock garden.

Event 5: Mr. Tanimoto runs into the street and sees panicked people and a squad of soldiers.

Event 6: The sky darkens.

PAGE 142: The bar graph gives you statistical data on the deaths in WWII; these numbers do not appear in the text. In addition, the bar graph breaks down this information by country, while the text mentions only the number of lives lost in the Soviet Union, grouping the other losses into one number. Last, the bar graph breaks down the numbers of lives lost in each country into civilians and soldiers. Again, the text lumps all losses into one number.

PAGE 143: Students will chose different types of information to display in their own graphics. Some examples of new graphics include: a bar graph or table of just civilian losses or just military losses; a graph or table of losses arranged from greatest to smallest; or a graph or table of Axis losses versus Allied losses.

PAGE 145: Paragraph 2: on August 6, 1945; soon

Paragraph 3: immediately after; on August 9; same day

Paragraph 4: next day; late August; on September 2, 1945

PAGE 146: Students' webs will vary, as will their summaries. Following is a sample web:

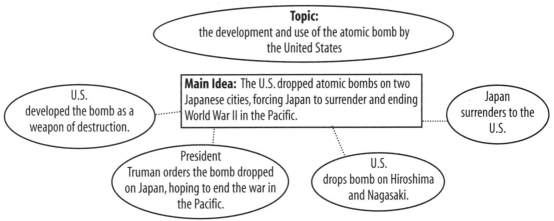

Topic:
the development and use of the atomic bomb by the United States

U.S. developed the bomb as a weapon of destruction.

Main Idea: The U.S. dropped atomic bombs on two Japanese cities, forcing Japan to surrender and ending World War II in the Pacific.

Japan surrenders to the U.S.

President Truman orders the bomb dropped on Japan, hoping to end the war in the Pacific.

U.S. drops bomb on Hiroshima and Nagasaki.

PAGE 150: Students will offer various bits of information about Mo Vaughn. Here are examples:

Number: 42

Team: Red Sox

Weight: 220 pounds

Info about player as a rookie: Sent to majors and then back to minors before returning to the majors and becoming an All-Star.

Interests: rap music; motivating kids to succeed, visiting sick kids

PAGE 154: Students' statements will vary but should center on de Vinck's love and compassion for his brother Oliver. The author felt that Oliver was an important, powerful part of his family; he wanted other people to recognize Oliver as special.

PAGE 155: Students' charts will differ. Following is one example:

detail: Oliver's family cared for him, feeding him and changing his clothes, diapers, and bed linen.	**de Vinck's main idea:** Although Oliver had disabilities, he was a powerful person, influencing his family and causing them to realize the true meaning of love.	**detail:** The author chose his future wife based on her reaction to Oliver.
	detail: Oliver's parents decided to care for him at home and not leave him in an institution.	**detail:** Oliver was a peaceful presence, and the family felt blessed to have him.

These details display how the family felt about Oliver, how his presence affected their lives (showing his "power," even how he affected de Vinck's choice of a wife).

PAGE 159: Students' charts will vary, as will their personality profiles. Following is a sample chart:

What I know about Bitton-Jackson	What I've inferred about Bitton-Jackson
She was imprisoned during the Holocaust when she was 14 years old.	She has a survivor's personality.
She survived and was liberated by American soldiers.	She's a very determined person.
She saw many people who suffered terribly.	She is hopeful that the cruelty of the Holocaust will not reoccur.
She is older now, a grandmother returning to the German town where she was imprisoned.	She has a vivid memory of the bad times she lived through.
	She is not happy to celebrate those times with a party, but would rather sit quietly and reflect on them.

PAGE 160: Students should write of Bitton-Jackson's determination to tell her story so that no one will forget what really happened. She is certain that if people know the truth of the Holocaust, their knowledge will help them keep crimes of intolerance from happening again.

PAGE 163: Students can make a case for Steinbeck's language being informal, but it is, for the most part, formal. There is a fair amount of complex vocabulary ("plaintively," "rigidity"), and he uses longer sentences, indicating a formal style. However, he also uses less complex words as well, and he starts several sentences with "and" or "but," indicating components of an informal style.

Although Steinbeck's writing is very descriptive ("savage, secret, dangerous melody"), and he does use some sensory language ("whistled," "glistened," and "moist"), this is not a major component of his style in this piece.

PAGE 164: Cofer's style is much more informal than that of Steinbeck, and her word choices are simple. Her sentences are long, and some have many clauses. She uses some sensory language ("brown," "plunged its claws deep into my skin") but not as much descriptive language.

Students' Venn diagrams will differ and should include some of the word choices and points mentioned above.

PAGE 165:   Following is a sample chart:

	Steinbeck	Cofer
long sentences		X
short sentences	X	
a lot of dialogue		
a little dialogue		
no dialogue	X	X
a lot of description	X	
a little description		X
figurative expressions used	X	X
no figurative expressions used		
suspenseful tone	X	
casual tone		X

PAGE 166:   See the answers for pages 163–165 for a description and comparison of Steinbeck's and Cofer's styles. Steinbeck's shorter sentences and more complex words heighten the tension in his story, while Cofer's informal language and long sentences fit a young girl's speech patterns.

PAGE 169:   *Beginning:* Yankees arrive at the house. The Master and Mistress gather everyone for a meeting.

Climax: Brother Solomon confronts the Master and asks for a school and some land for each former slave.

Resolution: The Master agrees to Brother Solomon's requests. An elderly woman worries about her future, and Brother Solomon says they will all take care of each other.

Hansen's structure, a letter, lets us into Patsy's thoughts about what's happening in the story. At the beginning of the story, Patsy is still a slave. She writes of doing her chores but not about how she feels. She does not know or reflect on how the soldiers' appearance will affect her future.

At the end, her tone is a little wry, speculating on being punished for taking advantage of her new freedom. Nevertheless, she can't wait to do so, and she looks forward to learning to read and write. We now see a bit more of who she is and what she wants. The soldiers' visit and the freedom they've given her also allows her to write more freely.

PAGE 170:   Students may mention that the structure of the poem looks like the leaf—carried on the wind, all alone, and helpless against that wind, until it hits the ground.

PAGE 172:   Students will say different about this poem, but most charts will look like this:

Stanza	Structure
1	Two lines, one is a question. The other is only one word. Both lines are dialogue.
2	Same as Stanza 1.
3	Same as Stanza 1.
4	Same as Stanza 1.
5	Two lines, one statement. No dialogue. Speaker is perhaps talking to himself or herself.
6	Three lines, a statement that is not finished in this stanza. No dialogue.
7	Two lines, a continuation of Stanza 6.
8	Three lines, two of which are one word each. No dialogue.

Chang's message is that she is not simply Chinese or American, but Chinese American. She says yes to being both, because she feels that she IS both, not one or the other. The importance to her of saying yes to both a Chinese identity and an American identity is emphasized by the number of one-word lines in the poem that contain "yes." It's short and sweet, and there's no ambivalence as in Stanza 6.

PAGE 173: Here are some sample criteria students may list for style:

sentence length

sentence structure

word choice

tone

use of dialogue

use of figurative language

Some sample criteria for structure:

choice of format (letter, poem, narrative)

line length

physical look of the poem (Are all the lines centered? What kind of picture does the poem look like?)

use of repeated elements

use of unusual punctuation or capitalization

PAGE 176: Students' answers will vary but should note that the word "Nobody" is capitalized. By capitalizing the word, the speaker shows that he or she is actually "Somebody," even if it's just in his or her own mind.

PAGE 177: Again, students will have different interpretations of the poem. One might say that Dickinson's message is this: Everyone is a "Somebody," whether or not they're well known.

The question marks at the beginning of the poem indicate that the speaker is a bit tenuous in her feelings about being Nobody. Once the speaker finds a friend who is also "Nobody," the tone of the poem perks up and becomes a little more resolute and prideful.

PAGE 179: Students will offer different reasons for Whitman's use of this rhyme and rhythm, including:

• The longer lines explain the story, what's happened up to this point. The shorter lines emphasize the mindset of the speaker, who cannot seem to understand that the captain is dead.

• The pattern of the repeated words emphasizes the action of the speaker trying to convince himself that the captain has actually died and cannot hear him.

Students' charts will vary. Following is an example:

Repeated word	Effects of Repeating the Word
Captain	Sounds like speaker is calling someone who's lost or gone far away, over and over, as if he can't believe the captain has really died
Bells	Even though bells ring for joy at their homecoming, by the end are ringing the death knell; emphasizes mournful tone of the poem
Heart	Sounds like the bell tolling
Fallen cold and dead	Emphasizes the finality of death

PAGE 181: Romeo and Juliet are playfully discussing whether or not to kiss. Romeo flatters Juliet, calling her "a holy shrine." She is reticent and instead would like to simply touch hands. He then asks her why. Juliet answers that their lips are used for prayer. He counters that lips and hands can both pray. He will pray that he can kiss her. She says that saints do grant prayers, so he playfully warns her of his kiss.

PAGE 182: 1. Sonnets have 14 lines.

2. There are three quatrains, and the couplet comprises the last two lines of this passage.

3. This sonnet does follow the pattern. In the quatrains, Romeo and Juliet carry on a playful debate about whether or not to kiss; in the last two lines, Juliet offers a final thought, and Romeo tells her that he will then kiss her.

4. hand, stand; this, kiss; much, touch; this, kiss; too, do; prayer, despair; sake, take.

Sonnets are an easy pattern to remember.

Because of the length, it is easier to work with a sonnet than other more complicated poetry patterns.

A story is easy to tell in the sonnet format.

A sonnet can stress a point.

PAGE 186: Students will choose different formats for their comparisons. Here is one example:

	Sonnets	Haiku	Free Verse
Length	14 lines	3 lines	No set length
Structure	3 quatrains, 1 couplet	1st line has 5 syllables, 2nd line has 7 syllables, 3rd line has 5 syllables	No set structure
Rhyming scheme	ABAB CDCD EFEF GG	None	None

PAGE 189: Students' wording will vary but should indicate that Lincoln thought that the men who fought at Gettysburg were brave heroes defending an important cause. That cause had not been completely realized.

PAGE 194: Some words that students might choose include purposeful, determined, serious, positive, warning, and hopeful.

PAGE 195: Students' organizers will vary. Following is a sample:

King	Lincoln
Tone: determined warning hopeful Viewpoint: Black people are not treated as equals to white people and are tired of the discrimination they experience. He hopes no one will use violence to achieve equality, but everyone needs to be prepared that some people might turn to violence.	Tone: respectful solemn Viewpoint: The men who fought at Gettysburg were brave heroes defending an important cause. That cause is not yet won and is still in need of defense ("unfinished work").

PAGE 199: Students will have different opinions of Kennedy's speech. Following are examples of personal experiences he used in his speech:

He cited his brother's assassination by a white man.

He quotes from a poet whose works he's read.

He says, "We've had difficult times," as everyone has.

PAGE 201: Students will offer various reasons for Kennedy's brainstorming in the speech. In actuality, Kennedy found out about King's death just before leaving for a scheduled campaign stop in Indianapolis. He was shocked and obviously had no speech prepared to address such a tragic event, but he decided to go and speak anyway. He had to brainstorm ideas as he spoke to the crowd that gathered to hear him.

PAGE 206: Writers might use humor in their work for the following reasons:

1. to catch the reader's attention

2. to soften the point they're making

3. to entertain the reader

4. to make a point

PAGE 209: The pilot's story is somewhat believable in that there could be alligators in the water. However, several aspects are obviously enhanced, such as the sheer numbers of alligators he implies roam the water and his theory that alligators know when police boats are coming.

Students' opinions of the pilot will vary, but many will probably say that his stories let the reader know that the pilot will be an unreliable witness in the remaining part of the text.

PAGE 212: Students may offer different opinions of Twain's point here, but they should include that he may have been poking fun at the way people of his own time dressed and acted (the late 1800s, the Victorian era). They wore so many pieces and layers that they couldn't move freely or be completely comfortable.

Humorous phrases in this passage include:

• "Well, a man that is packed away like that is a nut that isn't worth the cracking, there is so little of the meat, when you get down to it, by comparison with the shell."

• "He was going grailing, and it was just the outfit for it, too."

• "You don't get on your horse yourself; no, if you tried it you would get disappointed."

• ". . . I wanted to get down and settle with mine, but it wouldn't answer, because I couldn't have got up again."

All of these passages make fun of the folly of duels and in dressing in so many layers and so many pieces of clothing that restrict movement and make one look ridiculous.

PAGE 215: Students' impressions of Huck will differ, but following are a few points:

• Huck likes to live free and finds living with the widow and society's rules restrictive and against his nature.

• He has no interest in history and what has come before him; he lives in the present.

• He likes excitement and change. He finds living with the widow boring because there is no change.

• He doesn't like that the widow isn't open-minded enough to let him smoke (he hates that she doesn't like what she doesn't know). However, although he tries everything the widow throws his way, he isn't very open-minded about the value of what she wants to teach him.

• He sees no real value in education and does not try hard to learn new things, such as history or spelling.

Students' perceptions of the value of Twain's humor to the story will vary.

PAGE 217: Students will have varying things to say about Twain based on the letters. Some comments might include that he has a tongue-in-cheek sense of humor that borders on sarcasm at times. He also has a very affectionate and compassionate side to his nature, which shows in the loving way he discusses his cat's behavior.

I n d e x

Teacher's Guide page numbers are in parentheses following pupil's edition page numbers.

L e s s o n   T i t l e   I n d e x

L i t e r a t u r e   I n d e x